SHAKESPEARE'S WORLD

SHAKESPEARE'S WORLD

* * *

Edited by

James Sutherland and Joel Hurstfield

London
Edward Arnold (Publishers) Ltd.

First published 1964

Printed by W. & J. Mackay & Co. Ltd., Fair Row, Chatham, Kent

Contents

Preface

THE nine lectures in this volume were given at University College, London, to commemorate the fourth centenary of the birth of Shakespeare. For over a century University College has been a major centre for studies in Tudor history and literature. A. F. Pollard and Sir John Neale, W. P. Ker, R. W. Chambers, and C. J. Sisson all taught and worked here, and Sir Walter Greg was for many years an honorary lecturer in Bibliography in the English department. It was, too, an old student of the College, F. J. Furnivall, who founded the New Shakspere Society, and who first suggested, and helped to edit, the *New English Dictionary* which has played so important a part in the editing of Shakespearian texts.

The opening lecture was given by the Provost, himself an old student of the College, with the Chairman of the College Committee, the Rt. Hon. Lord Strang, another old student, in the Chair. The remaining lectures were given by present and past members of the English and History departments, with the exception of that delivered by Professor Geoffrey Bullough of King's College, London, who kindly responded to our invitation to speak on the Histories. Within the limitations of a short course of lectures, it was our aim to place Shakespeare in his own age, to deal with some of the major aspects of his work and with his critical reputation, and to address ourselves to a public that was by no means drawn exclusively from students of the period. The unusually large audiences which continued to attend these lectures throughout the course lead us to hope that those aims were realized.

Quotations from the plays and poems are given in a modernized spelling, and the text is that of the 'Globe' edition. The one exception is Dr. Hilda Hulme's lecture on 'Shakespeare's Language', where, for obvious reasons, she has adhered to the spelling of the First Folio.

J.H.
J.S.

University College, London
December 1963

I

Shakespeare's World

IFOR EVANS

As far as posterity is concerned the two most important men in Shakespeare's world were John Heminge and Henry Condell; fellow actors and old friends, they completed seven years after his death, for publication in 1623, the Folio edition of his Plays. What they did was not customary. Jonson had been an exception when he issued a Folio of his own Works in 1616 and had been teased by Heywood for so doing:

> Pray tell me Ben, where does the mystery lurk,
> What others call a play you call a work.[1]

Heminge and Condell may have been disturbed by Thomas Pavier's attempt, with William Jaggard as printer, to issue ten plays, not all by Shakespeare, as if they were his *Works*. This the King's Men, Shakespeare's old company, were able to prevent, though the plays were published separately as quartos. But the main motives of these two busy men must have been esteem and admiration for their recently dead companion. There are thirty-six plays in the Folio, and if anyone wishes to say that one or another of them is not by Shakespeare let him prove it.

Over the centuries critics have not been overgenerous to these remarkable companions of Shakespeare's years in the theatre. Eighteenth-century editors were patronizing. Some even doubted if these actor-editors were literate enough to write the prefaces to their Folio edition. With all this, it is interesting to contrast the respect shown by the doyen of Shakespearian bibliographers, Sir Walter Greg, and his appreciation of the editorial difficulties

[1] Ben Jonson, *Works*, ed. C. H. Herford and P. Simpson, vol. ix (1950), p. 13.

under which these men of the theatre laboured. But even if their achievement had not been commendable editorially the greatest debt would still be due to them, for, without the First Folio, knowledge of nearly one half of Shakespeare's work would be lost. Had they not prepared their edition, we should have no record of eighteen plays, including in tragedy no *Macbeth, Coriolanus*, and *Antony and Cleopatra*, and no *Twelfth Night, As You Like It* or *The Winter's Tale* in comedy, and no *Cymbeline. Pericles* was the only play now claimed for Shakespeare that they omitted. Perhaps they thought it not solely his or the texts too bad.

That the preservation of so many of his plays is owed to members of his own company emphasizes that the world of Shakespeare's maturity was the theatre. Stratford born, and with some years that history has not disclosed, it is clear that ultimately he came to London, possibly in 1584, and worked as an actor and an apprentice playwright. In the following years, until the Globe was burnt on 29 June 1613 during the first performance of *Henry VIII*, the theatre dominated his working life. The pressure must have increased when in 1594 he joined the Lord Chamberlain's Men, the leading company of the age. He was not only an actor, but the main playwright, and, as one who had a share in the Fellowship, he had also to assist in the company's business. He was no leisurely poet, living in a library, with time for contemplation and large and generous reading, and composing only when he felt so inclined. He had to write rapidly and constantly for a company continuously avid for new plays. Around him was ever the illimitable distraction and agitation of rehearsals.

The strain of theatrical business must have increased when the Lord Chamberlain's Men opened the new Globe Theatre in 1599. On James I's arrival in London, they entered into the king's service as the King's Men and indeed wore the king's livery; and many were the official calls on their talents, while Shakespeare's plays were frequently 'preferred' for performance at Court. The pressure mounted once again and in a more disturbing way when the company, in addition to the Globe, operated at the closed-in theatre at Blackfriars. Throughout all these years Shakespeare wrote in the intimacy of a group, knowing the talents and limitations of his companions: tragic roles for Richard Burbage, comedy for William Kemp, and later more subtle comic roles for Robert Armin.

Coleridge has described how the strength of a genius can be assessed by an ability to conceive ways of life remote from his own. Coleridge was writing, not of the plays, but of *Venus and Adonis*, but the argument holds: 'A second promise of genius is the choice of subjects very remote from the private interests and circumstances of the writer himself. At least I have found, that where the subject is taken immediately from the author's personal sensations and experiences, the excellence of a particular poem is but an equivocal mark, and often a fallacious pledge, of genuine poetic power.'[2] This power of imagination allowed Shakespeare to define his world of English history and his Roman world and the stranger territories of *Hamlet, Macbeth,* and *Lear* and many areas of fantasy. Yet, even when this imagination is exercised in a most absolute form, he is never far from the theatre and its problems. Into the magic of *A Midsummer Night's Dream* he found room to insert a dramatic presentation by the rustics, and the contemporary appropriateness of their efforts is shown when Bottom learns that his play has been 'preferred' by the Duke. Bottom's final instructions to his actors (IV. ii. 35ff.) must echo those which Shakespeare had often heard in the theatre: 'All that I will tell you is, that the Duke hath dined. Get your apparel together, good strings to your beards, new ribbons to your pumps; meet presently at the palace; every man look o'er his part; for the short and the long is, our play is preferred.'

Choice in such matters is always personal, but it might be urged that the most beautiful of his lyrics is in *Cymbeline* (IV. ii. 258ff.):

> Fear no more the heat o' th' sun,
>   Nor the furious winter's rages;
> Thou thy worldly task hast done,
>   Home art gone, and ta'en thy wages.
> Golden lads and girls all must
> As chimney-sweepers come to dust.

The lyric is the epitaph that the sons of Cymbeline, disguised under the names of Polydore and Cadwal, were to sing over the seemingly

[2] *Biographia Literaria*, ed. J. Shawcross, 1907, vol. ii, pp. 14–15.

dead body of Imogen. But when the parts were distributed Shakespeare found, what he always dreaded, that the boys' voices were cracked and around his beautiful lyric he had to write the following apologetic lines. Cadwal says:

> And let us, Polydore, though now our voices
> Have got the mannish crack, sing him to th' ground.

To which Polydore replies:

> Cadwal,
> I cannot sing. I'll weep, and word it with thee;
> For notes of sorrow out of tune are worse
> Than priests and fanes that lie.

Cadwal, resignedly, answers: 'We'll speak it then.'

Wherever he stretched his imagination the world of the theatre remained his constant preoccupation. Not only did he return from the world of the imagination to the theatre, he often made the theatre, where he spent all the years of his London life, sustain his imagination. The theatre thus entered frequently and profoundly into his imagery. The actor who forgot his lines was as much an anxiety as the boy-player whose voice cracked, and against neither failure was there any defence. So when Coriolanus is succumbing to the pleadings of Virgilia and Volumnia it is to the actor who has 'dried-up' that Shakespeare turns to interpret the situation (V. iii. 40ff.):

> Like a dull actor now,
> I have forgot my part, and I am out,
> Even to a full disgrace.

A multiplicity of references could be quoted to show how deep and constant was this preoccupation with the theatre, yet his attitude to actors themselves is not easy to understand. Probably, as an actor and a dramatist he had two separate approaches. That he was beloved in his own company of players seems amply proved: Heminge and Condell's tribute in producing the First Folio and their prefatory comments are evidence enough for that. It was as an author that they praised him; 'as he was a happie imitator of Nature, [he] was a most gentle expresser of it'. Yet though he had this genial relation with members of the Fellowship, the author in him is often irritated by the arrogance of actors, 'the robustious periwig-pated fellows', ignorant and unable to understand the finer shades of his intentions.

In the middle of a scene in *Troilus and Cressida*, which contains Ulysses' great speech on 'degree', possibly the most intricately philosophical speech in Shakespeare, Ulysses tells Agamemnon of Achilles (I. iii. 152ff.):

> Thy topless deputation he puts on,
> And, like a strutting player, whose conceit
> Lies in his hamstring, and doth think it rich
> To hear the wooden dialogue and sound
> 'Twixt his stretch'd footing and the scaffoldage—
> Such to-be-pitied and o'er-wrested seeming
> He acts thy greatness in; and when he speaks,
> 'Tis like a chime a-mending.

This conception of the actor's inadequacy returns again and again. Macbeth, when he hears of the death of Lady Macbeth, says with great dramatic appropriateness, 'She should have died hereafter', but he adds the memorable and reflective passage concluding with the lines (V. v. 24ff.):

> Life's but a walking shadow, a poor player
> That struts and frets his hour upon the stage
> And then is heard no more.

Maurice Baring in one of his *Diminutive Dramas* suggested that Burbage felt that the single line 'She should have died hereafter' did not give him sufficient scope, and that Shakespeare had to add the further speech in rehearsal, and with the actor there before him he indulged in a reflection on the acting profession. It is a pretty fancy. Those who feel that Shakespeare pursued more complex and philosophical themes within the plays see this as the climax of Shakespeare's insistence on Time in the tragedy. Whichever view is true, it was from the theatre that Shakespeare drew the substance of his comment.

A dramatist who obviously had a genius that the stage of his time could not fully contain must have had moments of high frustration, but, on a personal basis, for actors as fellow members of his profession he had only kindliness. The most moving passage is in *Hamlet*, Act II. ii. 554ff., when the Prince tells Polonius how to take care of the players: 'Do you hear, let them be well used; for they are the abstracts and brief chronicles of the time'. And when Polonius says that he will 'use them according to their desert', Shakespeare employs a phrase to recur in *Lear*: 'Use every man after his desert, and who shall 'scape whipping? Use them after your own honour and dignity.'

In this visit of the players in *Hamlet* Shakespeare illustrated, in a most audacious form, the degree to which the theatre dominated his life. The whole forward sweep of events is held up so that Shakespeare through Hamlet and Polonius should set out some of his own views of actors, of the stage, and the art of drama in general. Mrs. Nowottny will show that these discussions have ultimately a close relation to the theme of the tragedy and its action, but one may be permitted to wonder whether this excursion into dramatic criticism would have been so long and so entertaining if Shakespeare were not so completely enjoying himself. It is an ironic reflection that this great age of the English theatre was not, unlike later ages, weighed down by dramatic criticism. If Shakespeare had been encumbered by the mass of academic criticism that now surrounds his plays he could not have written two plays a year. It was a happy age of creation in the drama not of dissertation. Yet, obviously, Shakespeare reflected on his art, and here with a gracious effrontery he expanded on his own views in the middle of *Hamlet*, a tragedy whose theme was already overloaded. Where else in the whole of our drama does a writer appropriate the moment of high tragedy for an excursion on how plays should be written and performed? For this talk on plays and the drama is followed by the most moving of the soliloquies:

> O what a rogue and peasant slave am I!

His whole thinking about drama enters into these passages: the audiences that did not understand (''twas caviare to the general'); in one brief phrase he sums up the theme of the debate on the unities ('scene individable or poem unlimited'), and expresses his own decision to follow no law in drama beyond allowing the theme to hold all it can contain ('the law of writ and the liberty'). There was even room for the topical theatrical controversy about the companies of boy players ('an aery of children, little eyases, that cry out on the top of question'), and, of course, when Hamlet comes to address one of the players there is another reference to Shakespeare's constant fear for the voices of the boys in his own company: 'Pray God, your voice, like a piece of uncurrent gold, be not cracked within the ring.'

He reflected in the plays not only on the actors but on the theatre itself. The Chorus in *Henry V* gives his comment on the inadequacy of the material resources of the Theatre:

> And so our scene must to the battle fly;
> Where—O for pity!—we shall much disgrace
> With four or five most vile and ragged foils,
> Right ill-disposed in brawl ridiculous,
> The name of Agincourt. Yet sit and see,
> Minding true things by what their mockeries be.[3]

As he felt the strength of his art growing within him he contemplated the difference between the stage and life. At times he seems to have felt himself a captive within the theatre; as indeed he was. The company needed plays and he would give them, but at a certain period he was conscious of an art stronger than the players could sustain. The fact that *Hamlet* and *Lear* are far too long for performance in the Elizabethan theatre is some proof of this. Let them cut what might be necessary, he would write himself out. Some have discovered a mood of despondency with the whole of the theatrical art in the Sonnets:[4]

> Alas, 'tis true I have gone here and there
> And made myself a motley to the view,
> Gored mine own thoughts, sold cheap what is most dear,
> Made old offences of affections new.

Or again:

> O, for my sake do you with Fortune chide,
> The guilty goddess of my harmful deeds,
> That did not better for my life provide
> Than public means which public manners breeds.
> Thence comes it that my name receives a brand,
> And almost thence my nature is subdued
> To what it works in, like the dyer's hand.

As he went from his house or lodgings to the theatre this contrast

[3] Prologue to Act IV.
[4] Sonnets, cx, cxi.

between the bustling, active, real life and the shadow life of the theatre seems to have been frequently in his mind. 'Shadow' and 'fancy' were words to which he frequently returned. When Hippolyta complained that Bottom's play was the 'silliest stuff' Theseus was given the reply (V. i. 215ff.): 'The best in this kind are but shadows; and the worst are no worse, if imagination amend them.' Again it was to Theseus that he gave the bold definition of imagination (V. i. 14):

> And as imagination bodies forth
> The forms of things unknown, the poet's pen
> Turns them to shapes and gives to airy nothing
> A local habitation and a name.

One moving and subtle reflection on this contrast of imagination and reality follows Cleopatra's description of her dream in which she imagined that Antony was alive and a magnificent Antony. On ending her account she turns to Dolabella and asks (V. ii. 93f.):

> Think you there was, or might be, such a man
> As this I dream'd of?

When Dolabella replies 'Gentle madam, no', Cleopatra comments:

> But if there be, or ever were, one such,
> It's past the size of dreaming: nature wants stuff
> To vie strange forms with fancy; yet, to imagine
> An Antony, were nature's piece 'gainst fancy,
> Condemning shadows quite.

What was the background of this man who spent his best years in the London theatre? The English with all their passion for biography and anecdote and gossip have been able to discover very little about his life. I have always cultivated the fancy that in his later years he made a bonfire in his Stratford orchard of all the biographical material he had available saying, 'And now you English people, since you cannot ferret out the details of my life, you will have to concentrate on my plays.'

Some assumptions one must make. He was a Stratford man and, though his effective years were spent in London, he always had Stratford in mind as a place to which he would retire, and he visited Stratford several times during the London years. Yet the meagre details of his family life in Stratford are of very little illumination in interpreting the plays. One assumes, and it is only an assumption, that he went to the Grammar School at Stratford. To some such place he must have gone to master the textbooks of grammar and rhetoric which he employed so freely. It was in such a school that he discovered his interest in language, which remained the main passion of his life and on whose manipulation so much that is best in his art depends. I should like to accept the story that for a time he was a schoolmaster. The authority is John Aubrey, the Restoration gossip-writer, and Aubrey can be inaccurate. But he said he had this story from Mr. Beeston, that is from William Beeston, the actor, whose father, Christopher, was a boy-player in Shakespeare's company and spent his adult life in the theatre. Whether a schoolmaster or not, words dominated him and they went on marching through his mind, at least until the day he left London. *Love's Labour's Lost*, which, despite some recent views, I still hold to be one of the earliest of the plays, and, rarely for Shakespeare, one with an original theme, is dedicated not to plot or characters but to language:

> Taffeta phrases, silken terms precise,
> Three-piled hyperboles, spruce affectation,
> Figures pedantical . . . (V. ii. 407ff.).

At some moment he must have come into contact with another world, more splendid than his Stratford home and the various lodgings and houses where he lived as an actor in London. As he dedicated his two poems *Venus and Adonis*, 1593, and *The Rape of Lucrece*, 1594, to the Earl of Southampton, it would seem, without making any claim for a place for Southampton in the *Sonnets*, that it was in Southampton's house that he saw the life of nobility, with all its rich trappings and that the impression was profound. Dedications in the Elizabethan age had a conventional language all their own, but Shakespeare must have been announcing some degree of friendship when he wrote to the Earl of Southampton with *The Rape of Lucrece*: 'The love I dedicate to your Lordship is without end; whereof this pamphlet, without beginning, is but a superfluous moiety.' The poems and the sonnets showed that he was making claims, and successfully, to be considered as a serious man of letters, not a hack playwright. Robert Greene, Master of Arts of both Universities but a Bohemian belonging to the sordid life of London, had attacked Shakespeare in a passage, written allegedly on his deathbed, in 1592. He claimed that Shakespeare had put the scholar playwrights out of business. In the same year Henry Chettle, who was later to edit Greene's miscellaneous papers, made amends: he had met Shakespeare, he said, and found 'his demeanour no less civil than he excellent in the quality he professes. Besides divers of worship have reported his uprightness of dealing.'[5] Among the 'divers of worship' it might be possible to include Southampton.

The economics of the Elizabethan London theatre are difficult to understand, but when one adds Shakespeare's earnings as an actor to those as a playwright, and his share in the Fellowship, it is still difficult to realize how he could become so considerable an owner of property, not only in Stratford but at the gatehouse of the Blackfriars Priory in London. A story, not well founded, is told by Rowe, his first editor, on the authority of Sir William Davenant, that Southampton once gave Shakespeare 'a thousand Pounds to enable him to go through with a purchase which he had a mind to'.[6] The sum is incredibly large but not the gift itself, and he may have been assisted by a noble patron attached to that court which had so fired his imagination.

The rapidity with which his genius developed presents, it must be confessed, an insoluble problem. Explanations for the changes and the increasing depth of his art have been numerous. Some, it may be thought more sentimental, critics have emphasized biographical causes: the Dark Lady; the friend, with whom let us say his relation was complicated; the contact with the Earl of Essex, whose death on the block naturally led him to moods of pessimism and tragedy; the whole changing political atmosphere in Elizabeth's final years and in the early phase of James's reign. Yet close biographical identification with themes and motives in the plays can be exaggerated. He was much aware of what was happening in his time, and of the changes of temper and mood in his own age: life was

[5] Epistle to *Kind Heart's Dream*, published December 1592.

[6] See E. K. Chambers, *William Shakespeare: A Study of Facts and Problems*, 1930, vol. ii, pp. 266–7.

sufficiently intimate and compact for such things to be easily known. He was at the centre of things, but a shadow at the centre, realizing, as has been noted, that the stage is a shadow of reality. Whatever happened in the outside world one must come back to the fact that he was writing continuously, often under pressure, controlled only by the capacities and criticisms of the members of his company. His art developed by his own exercise of it, and from his increasing understanding of the possibilities of the instrument he employed.

From all this it might be argued that Shakespeare was less personally involved in all that his work exposes than later romantic critics have sometimes suggested. What affected him most was what happened inside the theatre. One could speculate that the most important event of his theatrical life was when his company moved from the open stage of the Globe, so completely adapted to his genius, to the closed-in stage of Blackfriars. Here, presumably, he tried *The Winter's Tale* and *The Tempest* and realizing that the changed and more elaborate conditions gave him no new worlds to conquer, he completed his arrangements to retire to Stratford, returning only at the plea of his fellow players for the first performance of *Henry VIII* on 29 June 1613, for that fateful night when, as already noted, the theatre was burnt down.

This assessment of his approach, which is difficult for the isolated and introspective modern artist to understand, is confirmed by his very practical and normal attitude to the personal problems of his own life. Though deeply engrossed in the business of the theatre, his mind was solidly involved, as soon as funds were available, in the purchase of properties in Stratford. Even in the years of the great tragedies he was pursuing his own rights in the courts, and in 1604, for instance, he sued Philip Rogers, an apothecary, for a debt of £1. 15s.[7]

There remains the problem of how the mere bulk of his production was achieved. He came to the English language at a uniquely happy time, when it was not yet too settled, and he had the genius to exploit that language to the full. In rapidity of composition, in making fuller use of his reading than better-read men have of theirs, and in genius, Keats can bear some comparison. But Keats worked in

[7] See E. K. Chambers, *op. cit.*, vol. i, p. 84; vol. ii, pp. 113, 118.

isolation, except for the admiration of a few friends. He lacked the exhilaration of a whole group of writers with similar aims working in genial emulation. Nor had he the quick prompting of the theatre and of a company of players who were his friends. Keats had also to do his best with a language which had been narrowed and codified since Shakespeare's day. Dr. Hilda Hulme[8] has illustrated this brilliantly. Shakespeare, for instance, unlike D. H. Lawrence, did not have to revive the plain, less seemly, words. They were in current usage, and generally understood. In her chapter, discreetly named, 'The Less Decent Language of the Time', she shows how Thomas Bowdler left some 'vulgar' and 'indelicate' expressions in his *Family Shakespeare* of 1818 because he did not know what the words meant, or rather what they meant to Shakespeare. Nor was it Bowdler alone, for, as Dr. Hulme says, 'earlier editors may well have credited him with a fullness of meaning to which they felt it unnecessary to draw attention. It is likely also that the eighteenth-century editors were aware of some implications in the Shakespearian text which, because of the narrower code of verbal decency imposed in Victorian times, no longer have a place in the ordinary language of protected academic life.' Many of us were brought up to believe that the emendation made by Theobald in 1733 in the hostess's description of the dying Falstaff was the most brilliant in the history of Shakespearian editorship. The Folio reads: 'for his Nose was as sharpe as a Pen and a Table of greene fields'. Theobald brought in sense and sentimentality with 'and a' babbled of green fields'. Dr. Hulme shows from current usage that the Folio text can stand, and that the hostess had a kindly bawdiness which more thin-lipped generations could not tolerate.[9]

Dr. Hulme's investigations are important, for they lead back to the central theme in Shakespeare's world that he was born at a time when the language was a ready instrument for genius and so he employed it. Blank verse was the ideal medium for that language and blank verse was less than half a century old when Shakespeare began to use it. Even in his own day his linguistic enterprise was recognized as the major achievement of his genius. One turns again to Heminge and Condell and to their preface, in the First Folio of 1623, 'To the

[8] *Explorations in Shakespeare's Language*, 1962, pp. 89ff.
[9] *Op. cit.*, pp. 93, 134ff.

great Variety of Readers':

> His mind and hand went together: And what he thought, he uttered with that easinesse, that wee haue scarse receiued from him a blot in his papers. But it is not our prouince, who onely gather his works, and giue them you, to praise him. It is yours that reade him. And there we hope, to your diuers capacities, you will finde enough, both to draw, and hold you: for his wit can no more lie hid, then it could be lost. Reade him, therefore; and againe, and againe.

The close, compact life of Elizabethan London must have been at every moment a stimulus. It was a manner of life which we in our remote, bureaucratic world cannot easily understand. It was far more physical and intimate in all senses of the term, with human experiences, at every moment, quickening the imagination. Death and danger were there present on the streets, and Shakespeare must have witnessed incidents involving them, even as he made his way to and from the theatre. Hamlet, as he dies, says (V. ii. 350ff.):

> Had I but time—as this fell sergeant, Death,
> Is strict in his arrest—O I could tell you—
> But let it be.

Shakespeare must have seen in the crowded London streets the sudden closing in of the law on its victim, and, as so often, he employed the immediate physical incident to illustrate his own abstract theme.

Every Elizabethan must have seen gibbets with bodies hanging exposed. For Shakespeare the experience registered at first in comedy. This has its importance, for the Elizabethan reaction to horror and violence and death was different from that of those who live in an age where the perils are more terrifying but remote, while the daily life is an enervating union of routine and of dull, bureaucratic complexity. So in *The Merry Wives of Windsor* (II. ii. 18f.) when Falstaff is denying Pistol a loan he says: 'At a word, hang no more about me, I am no gibbet for you.' Later, much later, when the mood changed, those dangling and exposed figures came back to feed the imagination in a different way. It was this London scene that gave the culminating moment to Cleopatra's wild speech of protest at her attempted arrest (V. ii. 56ff.):

> Rather a ditch in Egypt
> Be gentle grave unto me! rather on Nilus' mud
> Lay me stark naked, and let the water-flies
> Blow me into abhorring! rather make
> My country's high pyramides my gibbet,
> And hang me up in chains!

The combination of the immediate and the remote, 'the gibbet' and 'the pyramid', and, further, the combination no sooner conceived but made vitally metaphorical, these were the supreme qualities of Shakespeare's art.

In the narrow streets of London the courtier, the poet, and the 'mechanicals' could not avoid close contact, and Shakespeare registers vividly the physical impression that this made. He refers to it in kindly mood when Antony promises Cleopatra as a special pleasure, merely to wander through the streets (I. i. 53f.):

> Tonight we'll wander through the streets and note
> The qualities of people.

Often in the Roman plays, which give such a completely conceived picture of a Roman world, it is to the London scene that he returns for his imagery, and here the repugnance that the gentlefolk felt in their enforced contact with the 'mechanicals' is emphasized as Cleopatra described how she would be exposed as a captive in Rome (V. ii. 208ff.):

> . . . . mechanic slaves
> With greasy aprons, rules, and hammers, shall
> Uplift us to the view: in their thick breaths,
> Rank of gross diet, shall we be enclouded,
> And forced to drink their vapour.

The greater part of all this dramatic writing was done between early morning and sunset. Work at night there must have been, but light was bad and candles expensive, and after what was often a long day in the theatre weariness must have set in. Genius is the capacity of seizing out of your experience what is necessary for your art. Shakespeare had this in a supreme way. He made Autolycus describe himself as, 'a snapper-up of unconsidered trifles'. So did Shakespeare work that nothing in his experience capable of sustaining his imagination was ever forgotten. Even this very question of day and night, which we now solve with such mechanical ease, was exploited in his imagery. Only those who have lived outside civilization, and known the sudden coming on of night and the helplessness, even the fear that it engenders, can understand all that the contrast of day and night can mean. Shakespeare in *Romeo and Juliet* emblazons the night with the bold and extravagant image Romeo employs on the first meeting of the two lovers (I. v. 48ff.):

> O, she doth teach the torches to burn bright!
> It seems she hangs upon the cheek of night
> Like a rich jewel in an Ethiope's ear.

With a simplicity that he learned in his later years he gives to Iras the beautiful lines with which she addresses Cleopatra near the end of the tragedy (V. ii. 192f.):

> Finish, good lady; the bright day is done,
> And we are for the dark.

Even in his earliest plays, when rhetoric was elaborate enough to be a temptation, he dwelt on this awe-inspiring contrast of day and night. How profound was this experience of night can be seen in one of the most moving passages in *Macbeth* (II. i. 49ff.). There is, probably, still a Senecan element, but the imagination has been quickened to a new profundity:

> Now o'er the one half-world
> Nature seems dead, and wicked dreams abuse
> The curtain'd sleep; witchcraft celebrates
> Pale Hecate's offerings, and withered murder,
> Alarum'd by his sentinel, the wolf,
> Whose howl's his watch, thus with his stealthy pace,
> With Tarquin's ravishing strides, towards his design
> Moves like a ghost.

While his experience was thus held captive to his imagination, his reading was similarly exploited. T. W. Baldwin has shown[10] the textbooks and other volumes he must have read. I am in a minority in thinking that, except for the hidden years, his way of life would

[10] T. W. Baldwin, *William Shakespeare's Small Latine and Less Greeke*, 1944.

make extensive reading impossible. He had to memorize his parts, assist in the business of the theatre and in rehearsals, and, of course, he had to write the plays. Yet, unlike our own period, it was a time when cultivated men began early to read and regarded reading as one of life's main occupations. Yet, like Keats, he could hardly have achieved what he did had he not retained with the tenacity of genius all that could be of assistance to him as a creative writer. Most of his thought was unoriginal, but it was completely transfigured by the imaginative nature of his language. To quote a single example: it was W. P. Ker[11] who suggested that somewhere on Hamlet's tablets he had the phrase from Boethius: *Adeo nihil est miserum nisi cum putes*: and it was this that he recalled in addressing Rosencrantz (II. ii. 259f.):

> there is nothing either good or bad, but thinking makes it so.

If, then, one is to guess how his genius developed to such a depth and with continuous concentration, the more intelligible external factors are the nature of the language and of the times in which he lived. He was singularly fortunate, as has been suggested, to write before the language was completely settled at a time when there was much emulation among poets and dramatists in its bold use, when its employment was the major and most enjoyable of creative pastimes of the age. Further, the highest element in his genius was his language, obviously the main preoccupation of his life. No brilliance of production in a Shakespearian play can be effective if the words are mumbled or lost, and some modern actors would do well to bear this in mind. He came into a London that had intimacy, and wide areas of common understanding, before commerce had become dominant and bureaucracy with its contaminations had infected life into a complicated dimness. It was a world that had still some of the trappings of the medieval age, and yet was sustained into heightened experience by its own bold nationalism, and a consciousness of power. How fresh and exciting Elizabethan English could be appears in Queen Elizabeth's speeches, and Sir John Neale[12] has shown us that they are her own and not the product of some shadow writer.

[11] *The Dark Ages*, 2nd ed., 1955, p. 105.
[12] *Queen Elizabeth*, 1934, p. 383.

Her quality appears in the last address she made to the Commons: 'Of myself, I must say this: I never was any greedy, scraping grasper, nor a strict, fast-holding prince, nor yet a waster; my heart was never set upon any worldly goods, but only for my subjects' good. . . . It is not my desire to live or reign longer than my life and reign shall be for your good. And, though you have had, and may have, many mightier and wiser princes sitting in this seat, yet you never had, nor shall have, any that will love you better.'

With such a Queen the age and its poets had all encouragement to verbal exploits as daring as those of the Elizabethan voyagers. With Shakespeare it could be urged that the tumult of words at times overcame him and so stood between him and the drama. This is ultimately the criticism of Dryden and later of Johnson. 'A quibble', wrote Johnson in his *Preface to Shakespeare*,[13] 'is to Shakespeare what luminous vapours are to a traveller; he follows it at all adventures; it is sure to lead him out of his way, and sure to engulf him in the mire. . . . A quibble was to him the fatal Cleopatra for which he lost the world, and was content to lose it.' The Elizabethans with their livelier interest in language had a far greater respect for the pun than Johnson in the eighteenth century could conceive. As F. P. Wilson wrote: 'To an Elizabethan the play upon words was not merely an elegance of style and a display of wit; it was also a means of emphasis and an instrument of persuasion.'[14] But the pun was only the humblest instrument of an imagery that culminated in metaphor. Shakespeare had a supreme control of these imaginative identities in language which summon contrasting experience to illustrate a single idea. His struggle was to contain these cohorts of images, this vitally metaphorical language, within the confines of speech appropriate for a drama. That he became aware of the problem, in a conscious and self-critical way, cannot be doubted. The secret triumph of his art was his mastery of this great instrument of speech which seemed at first to have overwhelmed him. By the time of the great tragedies each play had a language proper to itself, with the atmosphere of the time, and an image of the spiritual conception in which the tragedy

[13] *Eighteenth Century Essays on Shakespeare*, ed. D. Nichol Smith, 2nd ed., 1963, p. 117.

[14] 'Shakespeare and the Diction of Common Life', *Proceedings of the British Academy*, 1941, vol. xxvii, p. 178.

centred. Here were the successes that the players did not fully understand, nor possibly even the audiences. He gave them all they could need, and then, as in *Lear*, something above all this, which was necessary to himself so that his own genius might be satisfied and his artistic integrity preserved.

II

The Elizabethan People in the Age of Shakespeare

JOEL HURSTFIELD

IN a famous sermon delivered at the court of King Edward VI in 1549, Hugh Latimer looked back over the years to his own early youth. He recalled to mind his father and remembered as a small boy helping him buckle on his armour when he went off to fight for King Henry VII against the rebels. His father, he says, was a yeoman: he had no land of his own, but leased some land for which he paid three or four pounds a year in rent. His father was able to maintain the family in a reasonable degree of comfort and, he goes on, he was able to pay for me to go to school 'or else I had not been able to have preached before the King's Majesty now'. For Latimer's sisters he was able to provide dowries and still had money left to give alms to the poor. Now, says Latimer, the man who rents the same land pays at least four times as much in rent and has nothing left for his children or even enough to give a poor man a drink at his door.[1]

The England which Hugh Latimer is describing is a society in process of dissolution. It is a time of rising prices, poverty, distress and social discord. This, in fact, is the society which existed in the two decades before William Shakespeare was born in 1564; two decades which saw more rapid social change than any other period in modern English history. I believe that the conditions of the twenty years which precede a man's birth set the pattern of his early thinking, and leave a permanent mark upon him. If this is so, then these unparalleled conditions of mid-Tudor England left their impress upon Shakespeare's mind, as they did upon the Elizabethan

[1] *Sermons of Hugh Latimer*, ed. G. E. Corrie, 1844, p. 101.

people as a whole. They did not, of course, *determine* Shakespeare's ways of thought—nothing could hold genius within the contemporary historical setting—but they provided some of the governing assumptions about society which intervened in his dramas, whether about ancient Rome, early Scotland, medieval England or Denmark. These assumptions were social instability, ideological conflict, a frequently re-enacted struggle for personal and political power. They included also the high optimism of national independence, identified especially with Henry VIII and Elizabeth, and the realization that independence and power were only gained and held by vigilance, and a constantly renewed struggle to survive.

Into what place and people was Shakespeare born? We are fortunate in having a detailed description of England sent home by the Venetian ambassador at the beginning of the sixteenth century.[2] 'The climate', he writes, '. . . is very healthy . . . and, though so far to the north-west, the cold in winter is much less severe than in Italy, and the heat proportionably less in summer. This is owing to the rain, which falls almost every day during the months of June, July and August; they have never any spring here, according to the report of the Islanders.' The country itself, he says, is 'all diversified by pleasant undulating hills, and beautiful valleys, nothing being to be seen but agreeable woods, or extensive meadows, or lands in cultivation; and the greatest plenty of water springing everywhere.'[3] With a population less than one tenth of what it is today, large tracts of the country had no more than scattered hamlets remotely connected with a distant small town.

Of the people themselves, he says that they are on the whole 'handsome and well-proportioned' although less handsome than the Scots. 'The English', he goes on, 'are great lovers of themselves and of everything belonging to them; they think that there are no other men than themselves, and no other world but England; and whenever they see a handsome foreigner they say that "he looks like an Englishman" and that "it is a great pity that he should not be an Englishman"; and when they partake of any delicacy with a foreigner, they ask him, "whether such a thing is made in their

[2] *A Relation . . . of England*, ed. C. A. Sneyd (Camden Soc., vol. xxxvii).
[3] *Ibid.*, pp. 8–9, 20.

country?" ' They like good food, he tells us, drink only a modest amount of wine and are fond of ale and beer. They dress well and speak courteously. Although their language, like Flemish, is derived from German it 'has lost its natural harshness, and is pleasing enough as they pronounce it'.[4] They are alert and intelligent and the educational opportunities for poor scholars are good. But they bring up their children toughly and with a 'want of affection' and board them out not later than the age of nine as pages, apprentices or servants. The English are justly famed as soldiers; the only trouble is 'that when the war is raging most furiously, they will seek for good eating, and all other comforts, without thinking of what harm might befall them'. He has some unkind things also to say about Englishmen as lovers. He says that he has never noticed anyone whether at court or among the lower orders to be genuinely in love, and concludes 'either that the English are the most discreet lovers in the world, or that they are incapable of love'. 'I say this of the men', he writes, 'for I understand that it is quite the contrary with the women, who are very violent in their passions.'[5] The ambassador thought that Englishwomen were very much under their husbands' thumbs. Fynes Moryson, a more shrewd observer of the contemporary scene, writing in the early seventeenth century, put things differently. 'England in general', he wrote, 'is said to be the hell of horses, the purgatory of servants and the paradise of women.'[6]

A lot of the ambassador's report is, of course, hearsay and exaggeration; but we catch in it some of the authentic echoes of the Tudor period, if of no later age: the belief, for example, that Englishmen should not wear their hearts on their sleeves or show affection to their children—Roger Ascham, the foremost educational reformer of Elizabethan times began writing his book, *The Scholemaster*, in order to ameliorate the severities of the school system. The immediate cause for his book, he tells us in the preface, was the news that some boys had run away from Eton for fear of being whipped. But it was extraordinarily difficult for a single observer to do justice to the mosaic of people and cultures compressed within one small island.

[4] *Ibid.*, pp. 20–22.
[5] *Ibid.*, pp. 23–25.
[6] Fynes Moryson, *Itinerary*, 1617, pt. 3, p. 53.

These, then, were the Elizabethan people: some sixty noblemen, of old or new lineage or—more likely—a mixture of both; a diffuse gentry class of varying fortunes; a substantial yeomanry, and a peasantry of fluctuating circumstances, above or below the subsistence level, many of them partially occupied in the textile industry. The Elizabethans were scattered very widely over the shires of England and Wales. Some continued to live in the ancient cities like York, Winchester or Exeter, with populations rarely exceeding 10,000; some in great ports like Bristol and Hull whose trading vicissitudes were generally attributed to the increasing grip of London and her Merchant Adventurers on the whole of English trade; many, too, lived on the sea as sailors or fishermen, and they were proud of their calling. 'Saint Patrick for Ireland', cried Thomas Nashe, 'Saint George for England and the Red Herring for Yarmouth'.[7] Many more lived in the textile areas, especially of East Anglia and the West Country. But the overwhelming majority lived on the land, growing crops and tending cattle and sheep, with some branch of the domestic cloth industry as a by-employment for themselves and their families. Mining and metallurgy were also becoming increasingly important.

In the towns there were the growing professional classes of lawyers, merchants, industrialists with their artisans and servants increasingly divorced from the soil. But the division between town and country had not yet come about. When Robert Cecil rose in Parliament and said: 'I do not dwell in the country, I am not acquainted with the plough', he was clearly speaking with a touch of irony.[8] The encloser of Hatfield Wood was surely not unacquainted with country pleasures. Every Englishman, wherever he lived, was within easy walking distance of green fields. Even Londoners, whose city was growing fast and had reached a population of about 200,000 by the end of the sixteenth century, could quickly walk into the country or visit fashionable villages like Hackney, Kensington or Chelsea. A glance at any map of London in Shakespeare's day shows extensive ribbon development along the Thames with its fine

[7] Cited in *Tudor Economic Documents*, 1924, ed. R. H. Tawney and E. Power, iii, 280.

[8] *Journals of all the Parliaments* . . ., ed. Simonds D'Ewes, p. 674.

churches, great houses and vastly overcrowded tenements—and beyond that lay open fields.

England had been a united nation for centuries; but in practice she remained a gathering of many regions still bearing the signs of the seven kingdoms of the early Middle Ages. Within the country local variation was enormous. When Sir Walter Ralegh got up in the House of Commons and spoke in his broad, rather harsh Devonshire accent, there were many who must have found it difficult to understand what he was saying, and of those who could understand him many who disliked what they heard. (The Sir Walter Ralegh of the history books is not the Ralegh known to Elizabethans—who saw him as able, ambitious, hot-tempered and untrustworthy—but the Ralegh of the heroic years when he sat in the Tower eating his heart out, experimenting in sciences and writing his history of the world.) But if there were these great varieties of speech, thought and life throughout England, it was at the Celtic border that the differences were sharpest. In Cornwall, a Celtic speech was still heard, but it was fast losing its hold. In Wales it possessed marvellous powers of survival. Cromwell's Statute of Wales of 1536 had had as one of its declared objectives the imposition of the English language upon the whole principality of Wales.[9] Since they

> do daily use a speech nothing like nor consonant to the natural mother tongue used within this realm, some rude and ignorant people have made distinction and diversity between the king's subjects of this realm and his subjects of the said dominion and principality of Wales, whereby great discord, variance, debate, division, murmur and sedition hath grown between his said subjects.

The statute was designed to extinguish the Welsh language. But, as in so much else, the Welsh people conquered their conquerors. Having given a dynasty to the English throne, and assimilated their native administration to the English shire system, the Welsh gentry sent their Members of Parliament and their children often to English schools. But their tongue and their Bible and their music remained Welsh, and they remained throughout the centuries loyal in their nonconformity. Their sister nation, the Irish, formed a tragic contrast. Divided against themselves and divided by their English

[9] 27 Hen. VIII. c. 26.

masters, the Irish struggled on in hopeless poverty and in a racial war made more bitter by religious persecution and economic exploitation. They lost everything except their identity. Their masters, too, lost heavily in a series of Pyrrhic victories which drained away scarce English treasure in the unfathomed bogs of Ireland. Scotland was outside the queen's dominions; and here English activities were divided between fishing in the troubled Scottish waters of religious intolerance and baronial feud, and shaping an alliance.

The Stratford and the Warwickshire in which Shakespeare grew to manhood lay geographically at the centre of England; and at the centre, too, of agrarian change. If Warwickshire included the forest of Arden and the rustic magic of a *Midsummer Night's Dream*, it too had its enclosures and evictions, its poverty and disorder, its religious discontents. If Warwickshire gave us Shakespeare, we might perhaps also remember that it gave us Robert Catesby, the brains behind Gunpowder Plot—if brains is the appropriate word. But the crisis of land and rent was undoubtedly the greatest crisis of all. Here is part of a prayer issued in 1553:

> We heartily pray thee, to send thy holy Spirit into the hearts of them that possess the grounds, pastures and dwelling places of the earth . . . that they, remembering the short continuance of their life, may be content with that that is sufficient, and not join house to house, nor couple land to land, to the impoverishment of other, but so behave themselves in letting out their tenements, lands, and pastures, that after this life they may be received into everlasting dwelling places: through Jesus Christ our Lord.
>
> Amen.[10]

The prayer book from which I have just quoted deals, of course, with eternal things. But we do not forget that it was set forth in 1553, at the height of the rent crisis and only four years after Ket's Rebellion, which had brought the East Anglian peasantry to arms, and which had toppled the Protector Somerset from power. It was only five years before Elizabeth came to the throne.

Under Elizabeth, after the re-coinage of 1561, inflation slackened somewhat but was never halted; and in 1578 a preacher at St. Paul's Cross, perhaps under government direction, urged his hearers not to

[10] Cited in *Tudor Economic Documents, ed. cit.*, iii, 62–63.

exaggerate the price rise. He referred derisively to the golden age in the past, when 'we lived as we lusted, priests were good fellows, adultery was borne withal, bread was bigger, ale was stronger, beef more plentiful, trouts fatter and better, all things cheaper, twenty-four eggs for a penny'.[11] On the contrary, so the argument runs, *these* were the better times: and they had never had it so good.

The roots of this relatively rapid social change are difficult to trace. They have been attributed to the Reformation which, it is said, made men set great store upon material things and therefore willing to oppress the poor for monetary gain. I have often seen this comforting *cliché* stated, but I have never seen any evidence to support it—and I know of a good deal which refutes it. The intruding Protestant landlord who bought up monastic land was sometimes no more harsh as a rent-collector than the departing Catholic abbot. The Reformation and the dissolution of the monasteries undoubtedly did severe cultural harm in the destruction of lovely monastic buildings and the treasures they housed. But we now know that the effects upon education have been vastly exaggerated. As for the belief that, with the coming of the Reformation Englishmen stopped helping the poor and began helping themselves, that, too, must take its place among the exploded fallacies of the period. Paris which remained Catholic had just the same social problems as London which went Protestant. But significant change, taking place in both trade and industry, intensified the heavy and disruptive pressures upon land; and, in all this, monetary inflation undoubtedly played its part. But the greatest force of all exerted upon the Tudor nation was the rise in population. In the period between the 1530s and the 1630s—roughly the generation before Shakespeare was born and Shakespeare's own lifetime—the population of England, which had been falling or stationary for almost two centuries, proceeded to double itself. We have no reliable statistics; but it can reasonably be said that when Shakespeare was born the population had already risen above three million and by the time that he died in 1616 it was in the neighbourhood of five million.

Compared with the population growth since the nineteenth century, all this seems modest enough; but taken in its contemporary

[11] M. M aclure, *The Paul's Cross Sermons*, 1958, p. 123.

economic context the population expansion of the Tudor period is impressive. For England in the mid-sixteenth century had a relatively underdeveloped economy: she was a producer of raw materials, largely wool, and an exporter of unfinished cloth. Her industries were primitive and sparsely distributed; her towns were small. Even her overseas trade was, to a large extent, in other men's hands. In such circumstances an expanding population exerted a severe pressure on the whole economy and way of life. For a primitive economy cannot easily absorb a rise in population when that rise is faster than the technical progress of industry—which is roughly the story of the West Indies today. Successive Tudor governments found to their dismay that they were faced with a population which could no longer be contained within the traditional framework of a medieval order. Here was a problem to be found all over western Europe at this time; and its causes we still do not wholly understand.

But its effects were visible enough. And Shakespeare must have heard the tramp of many feet in the Warwickshire lanes and must have seen the London mob in action, in search of work—or mischief—a constant source of anxiety to the governing classes of the city and of Westminster. 'You are thought here', says Dogberry to the second watch, 'to be the most senseless and fit man for the constable of the watch; therefore bear you the lantern. This is your charge:—you shall comprehend all vagrom men; you are to bid any man stand, in the prince's name.' 'How if a' will not stand?' asks the second watch. 'Why, then,' says Dogberry, 'take no note of him, but let him go; and presently call the rest of the watch together, and thank God you are rid of a knave.' 'If he will not stand when he is bidden,' says Verges, underlining this prudent advice, 'he is none of the prince's subjects.' (*Much Ado,* III. iii. 23ff.)

But Shakespeare elsewhere, and without the genial incompetence of Dogberry, shows us the mob in action as a political force, and an ugly, crude and insolent force it is. The men who—inflamed by Mark Antony's oratory—breathe fire and slaughter against Caesar's murderers whom so recently they have applauded; the men who slay Cinna the poet merely because he bears the same name as Cinna the conspirator; the bloody interplay between Coriolanus and the citizens of Rome: all these and other incidents show Shakespeare's intimate awareness of the power of the people and his deep distrust and fear of the exercise of that power. If we are looking for the first promise of popular democracy in the thought of Shakespeare, we shall look in vain. To Elizabethans the very word 'popularity', that is popular support, carried the dread overtones of popular discord and intestine war. We should never forget that Shakespeare's generation had ever present in its political memory the stories of what the Anabaptists had accomplished in Münster, when the extremists made a bid for the communal ownership of all things, established polygamy by law, and opened a reign of terror, surpassed only by the terror with which the movement was suppressed. To the Elizabethans popular rule was unthinkable; and one of the hardest things to forgive in the Earl of Essex was his 'popularity', that when he rose in 1601, he tried to carry the London mob with him—an open challenge to the government at Westminster. In *Henry IV* (III. ii. 63ff.) the king speaks contemptuously of Richard II, who

> Mingled his royalty with capering fools,
> Had his great name profaned with their scorns,
> And gave his countenance, against his name,
> To laugh at gibing boys, and stand the push
> Of every beardless, vain comparative. . . .

But though the Elizabethans believed that the people should keep their place, that does not mean that they oppressed the people. The Elizabethan Poor Law, as it emerged when finally consolidated at the end of the sixteenth century, although harsh to the persistent vagrant whether he could help it or not, displayed many progressive elements in its social thinking and set the pattern for a policy which endured for centuries. The Elizabethans believed in a balanced society in which, it was hoped, every man knew his place, and occupied it with some degree of comfort. The governing classes were both paternalistic and patronizing; and nowhere is this attitude better displayed than in the advice which that archetype of elder statesmen William Cecil, Lord Burghley—Shakespeare's Polonius—prepared for his son.[12]

> 8. Towards thy superiors be humble yet generous; with thy equals familiar yet respective; towards inferiors show much humility and some

[12] *Advice to a Son,* ed. Louis B. Wright, 1962, pp. 12–13.

> familiarity, as to bow thy body, stretch forth thy hand, and to uncover thy head, and suchlike popular compliments. The first prepares a way to advancement; the second makes thee known for a man well-bred; the third gains a good report which once gotten may be safely kept. . . . Yet do I advise thee not to affect nor neglect popularity too much. Seek not to be E. and shun to be R.[13]

The Elizabethan dream was of social order, articulated, well founded, socially established and secure. Any appeal to the people threatened the whole framework of internal peace and order. There is a famous passage from *Troilus and Cressida* (I. iii. 83ff.) in which Shakespeare, through the voice of Ulysses, is called as witness to the governing conservatism of the age:

> The heavens themselves, the planets, and this centre,
> Observe degree, priority, and place, . . .
> . . . How could communities,
> Degrees in schools and brotherhoods in cities,
> Peaceful commerce from dividable shores
> The primogenitive and due of birth,
> Prerogative of age, crowns, sceptres, laurels,
> But by degree stand in authentic place?
> Take but degree away, untune that string,
> And hark what discord follows! . . .

It is indeed a famous passage. But I think that it has been unduly emphasized. For I think that Elizabethans were more ready for social change than we have sometimes been inclined to recognize. It is true that they sometimes spoke of the different classes as though they were clearly defined and had the divisions permanently drawn; but, in fact, the reverse was the case. There was a great deal of social mobility; and men were easily accepted into a new class, provided that they assimilated the tastes and habits of those whom they joined. The College of Heralds did for the rising classes of the sixteenth century what the public schools provided in the nineteenth—the civilizing of new riches. 'As for gentlemen', wrote Shakespeare's contemporary, Sir Thomas Smith, quoting Harrison, 'they be made good cheap in England. For whosoever studieth the laws of the realm, who studieth in the universities, who professeth liberal sciences, and

[13] In some versions E. and R. are given as Essex and Ralegh.

to be short, who can live idly and without manual labour, and will bear the port, charge and countenance of a gentleman, he shall be called master, for that is the title which men give to esquires and other gentlemen, and shall be taken for a gentleman. . . . A king of heralds shall also give him for money arms newly made and invented, the title whereof shall pretend to have been found by the said herald in perusing and viewing of old registers . . . Such men are sometimes called in scorn gentlemen of the first head.'[14] 'Gentility', said Lord Burghley, 'is nothing but ancient riches.'[15] And I don't think that it was very ancient either: one generation was enough.

There was, then, in Elizabethan England, a good deal of movement from one class to another. Practice was far more flexible than theory; and it was the *arrivistes* who proclaimed most loudly the splendours of title, rank and tradition, and who most feared its decline. There is a pedigree at Hatfield House of Queen Elizabeth I which traces her ancestry back through King Arthur in a straight line and on to Adam; while Lord Burghley's pedigree, also at Hatfield House, is a tribute to the rich industry of the historian Camden at the expense of the harsh facts of history itself. Our English social system was, under the first Elizabeth, hierarchic—as it is under the second—with an elaboration of social distinction (to which we have since added distinction of speech); but it has never acquired the rigidity of a caste. It is caste not class which divides a nation to the point of self-destruction. It is the fashion to speak of the *nouveaux riches* as though their social influence is wholly harmful. Sometimes it is; but in many other cases it is they who have supplied the immense drive for cultural expression and experiment. For it is new wealth not ancient wealth which is more plentiful, more fluid and more eager and able to recruit artists and scholars in its own and the public service. It was the new men of Elizabethan England, the Cecils, the Russells, the Hattons and the Dudleys—rather than those of ancient and sometimes impoverished lineage—who summoned the artists and the architects and the playwrights and the poets to work for them and

[14] Sir Thomas Smith, *De Republica Anglorum*, ed. L. Alston, Cambridge, 1906, pp. 39–40.

[15] *Advice to a Son,* ed. Louis B. Wright, p. 10.

for posterity. Emmanuel College, Cambridge, of the sixteenth century, like Nuffield College, Oxford, of the twentieth, recalls to mind the pious ambitions of the new men of their age.

If the nation was socially mobile, it was also geographically mobile, more mobile than we used to think; and that was as well. For it was the continuous flow into London of the immense variety of people and talent which brought Shakespeare to the capital, and brought also the wonderful opportunities for him to exercise his art. When the economist, J. M. Keynes, said that England got Shakespeare when she could afford him, he was in fact saying that it was the concentration of wealth, population, power and leisure in the capital which allowed and encouraged the development of a flourishing theatre.[16] It may be true that poets write great poetry while starving in garrets (although we sometimes forget how much bad poetry is written by poets starving in garrets). But playwrights do not go on producing great plays unless men can afford to build theatres for them, and audiences can afford to go to the plays.

For if the capital and the countryside had plenty of examples of grinding poverty, starvation and disease, it displayed also much evidence of wealth, prosperity and comfort. The bare, damp, draughty medieval castles, irrelevant to the changed conditions of warfare, were giving place to the sturdy stateliness of the Tudor mansion, Holdenby, Hardwicke Hall, Longleat, Theobalds, and in the next reign, Hatfield House. In London, along the Strand and elsewhere, the great statesmen built or extended houses appropriate to their dignity and display: Cecil House, Leicester House, Essex House, Hatton House, places still commemorated in our London street names. Indeed, noblemen like the Earl of Leicester and his brother the Earl of Warwick, had their own 'men', that is troupes of actors, who could be called upon during the elaborate festivities of the age; and in one such troupe Shakespeare served his apprenticeship. Contemporaries like William Harrison speak of the rising standard of living which they have witnessed in their own lifetime, a rise which, he says, extends even to the peasantry. But it was unevenly and insecurely distributed: unemployment, war, famine, plague grievously reduced the precarious hold of the artisan or

[16] J. M. Keynes, *A Treatise on Money*, 1934, ii, 154.

village labourer on his slender means of subsistence and upon life itself. And for all classes, child mortality was extremely high; the expectation of life was short, and in sickness reduced still further by the old wives' remedies of superstition on the one hand or expert medical opinion on the other.

In spite of the wide differences in the standards of living, there was a certain cohesion about English provincial life. But one thing still divided the nation, namely religion. The generation preceding Shakespeare's birth had been the turbulent years of the English Reformation, when the nation swung back and forth, from Catholicism to Protestantism under Henry VIII; then on to extreme Protestantism, then back to Catholicism, and now under Elizabeth to a Janus-like State religion which had the double disadvantage of looking like Catholicism to the Protestants and Protestantism to the Catholics. A child born in 1533, the year when Elizabeth was born, had, if his family was conformist, subscribed to five different versions of the Christian religion by the time that he was twenty-six. When Shakespeare was born, the Elizabethan church settlement was only five years old. Like the throne itself it was manifestly and painfully insecure. It was a State Church made—so I believe—for political ends: to embrace as many as possible of those who were weary of the rancorous war of the theologians, who wished a plague on both their houses, who were good but not devout Christians, and who felt that the time had come for domestic peace.

How many people there were who held these temperate views was unknown to the Queen, as it remains unknown to historians; but clearly the Queen was one of them. To persuade her fellow countrymen to accept this State settlement—or to impose it upon them—became her lifelong mission. In one sense the mission failed: there were Catholics who preferred to die rather than give up their moral duty to convert their fellow countrymen to the true faith. There were some Protestants, or Puritans as they came to be called, who regarded the Elizabethan settlement as a travesty of what a Protestant Church should be; and they, too, preferred to die rather than yield. The Elizabethan Government never understood the nature of dissent, or if they did, felt that they could not accommodate it in the existing political situation. In political terms the Catholics were allied to a foreign authority which had condemned the Queen and called upon her subjects to rebel: to persecute the propagandists seemed therefore the only political policy that a responsible government at war could adopt; but, of course, it could not resolve the dilemma of the Catholic idealists. Yet it was not they but the Puritans who constituted the real danger. For the Puritans operated within the existing system, had powerful allies in high places, and by their theory, and ultimately their practice, made the whole concept of monarchy for a time untenable. A handful of Catholic extremists may have attempted to assassinate Queen Elizabeth, but it was in fact the Puritans who in due course plunged England into civil war and chopped off the head of a king.

Queen Elizabeth's aim, even though she did not continuously succeed in it, was to hold some central position, uncommitted to too precise a definition of dogma—it is interesting that the Puritans were sometimes called by their enemies *precisians*. Unlike her brother and her father, she had no skill or interest in theology. She tended to see religious problems in terms of national interest and the national survival.

All this was boldly stated to the Queen herself in a sermon by Edward Dering, the Puritan, a sermon which she never forgot or forgave. Of the religious issue, as he saw it, he said 'it toucheth not belike your commonwealth, and therefore you are so well contented to let all alone'.[17] *Your commonwealth!* The welfare of the State came first. I think that this attitude which I have described as Elizabethan—in the sense that it was the Queen's own attitude—was also Shakespearian. As a man of the theatre he can have had no great esteem for the Puritans; but he treats them briefly in his plays, *Twelfth Night* and *Measure for Measure*, and with imagination and compassion. We should remember, perhaps, that at this period, before Puritanism took on its most aggressive political form, it was a movement patronized in high places, by Leicester, Warwick, Burghley, Essex—although never, of course, by the Queen. Of the Catholics, too, Shakespeare could write with compassion, as of Katharine of Aragon in *Henry VIII* or the Friar in *Romeo and Juliet*.

[17] E. Dering, *Works*, 1597 ed., p. 27, discussed in Dr. P. Collinson's forthcoming *A Mirror of Elizabethan Puritanism* (Dr. Williams' Lecture, 1963).

But where he sees political ambitions as a threat to English national independence, then, as in *King John* (III. i. 152ff.), he makes the King's riposte to the cardinal, who comes threatening papal excommunication, a proud trumpet-call to defiance: 'Tell him this tale,'—[King John is sending back a challenge to the pope]

> and from the mouth of England
> Add thus much more, that no Italian priest
> Shall tithe or toll in our dominions;
> But as we, under heaven, are supreme head,
> So under Him that great supremacy,
> Where we do reign, we will alone uphold,
> Without the assistance of a mortal hand:
> So tell the pope . . .
> . . . . I alone, alone do me oppose
> Against the pope, and count his friends my foes.

The scene of the play is set in the early thirteenth century, but the reference is, of course, to the papal bull of 1570 deposing Elizabeth, and to the war with Catholic Spain in which Elizabeth was now heavily involved and whose end she would not live to see. The play was produced in 1598 in a dark period of the war, two years after the failure of the papal attempt to invade Ireland. And the passage that I have quoted must have brought the house down. Yet when we turn back a decade earlier to the Tilbury speech of Queen Elizabeth we find these anticipatory lines:

> I have the heart and stomach of a king
> And of a king of England too!
> And think foul scorn that Parma or Spain
> Or any prince of Europe,
> Should dare to invade the borders of my realm.

We think, too, of another age and another statesman, and of the Dunkirk defiance of 1940.

It is in Shakespeare's work that we meet over and over again that sense of nationhood, echoing the national mood and at the same time inspiring it, a nation still protected by the narrow waters of the channel, alone, confident, entering upon its political maturity.

It was that political maturity which was best displayed in the rising powers of the House of Commons. Peers and bishops sat in the House of Lords; but the Lower House was, of course, no popularly elected assembly based upon universal suffrage. Many of the borough representatives spoke for no one but themselves or a narrow local oligarchy, or were in the pocket of some lord or other patron; those sent by the shires, elected nominally by all the forty-shilling freeholders, in fact often came in as the result of force, fraud or some political horse-trading between rival factions. Yet these four hundred men who came to Westminster brought with them, in many cases, powerful notions of their social responsibilities. They believed that they must speak for their local community; and, as we read their speeches, we hear the authentic accents of provincial England. '. . . Every Englishman', wrote Sir Thomas Smith, 'is intended to be there present, either in person or by procuration and attornies, of what pre-eminence, state, dignity or quality soever he be, from the prince (be he king or queen) to the lowest person of England. And the consent of the parliament is taken to be every man's consent.'[18] Parliament was still far from the period of its supremacy: the Queen could summon and dismiss Parliament at her will. During many years it did not meet at all. It met, on an average, as Sir John Neale has shown, no more than three weeks a year.[19] But at a time when communications were bad, and men's concerns were intensely local and limited, Parliament, with all its weakness and private interests, was a unifying force for the nation.

But, of course, the greatest unifying force was the Queen. About her we know a great deal; but it is all too little. For she combined all the complexities of a renaissance monarch with the subtle and ambiguous charm of a sophisticated woman who had spent her life among sophisticated men. She was gay, generous, considerate, but was also disingenuous, moody, tempestuous and, at times, unaware or careless of the agony which her cruel wit could create. She was not beautiful and she knew it. But she had grace and dignity on all formal occasions; and these qualities she retained to the end. The Queen whom Shakespeare saw was the Queen as depicted in the Ditchley portrait of 1592, approaching her sixtieth year. It is the face of a woman who is confident, resolute, if a little tired, who has learned much from life and paid heavily for her lessons.

[18] *De Republica Anglorum*, p. 49.

[19] Based on J. E. Neale, *The Elizabethan House of Commons* (1949), p. 381.

But when we think of her our first thoughts turn not to the Ditchley portrait but to Shakespeare's play *Henry VIII* and the eulogy, in the dramatic form of a prophecy, which Cranmer speaks in the last scene (V. v. 33ff.). We notice that he speaks proudly of the Queen as a monarch; but he measures her by what she will achieve for the people of England:

> In her days every man shall eat in safety,
> Under his own vine, what he plants; and sing
> The merry songs of peace to all his neighbours.

But, during all the years of the Elizabethan period that Shakespeare spent in London, England was not at peace: to war was added famine, and after three desperate summers and three harvest failures, in 1596 in Oxfordshire, instead of the 'merry songs of peace' there was heard the tramp of the rebellious peasantry. And where of all places shall we find the best description of the cold, wet summers, the failed harvests, the empty granaries of these disastrous years? It is in *A Midsummer Night's Dream*, and from the mouth of Titania:

> The ox hath therefore stretch'd his yoke in vain,
> The ploughman lost his sweat; and the green corn
> Hath rotted ere his youth attain'd a beard;
> The fold stands empty in the drowned field
> And crows are fatted with the murrion flock; . . .
> No night is now with hymn or carol blest: . . .
> The seasons alter: hoary-headed frosts
> Fall in the fresh lap of the crimson rose;
> . . . the spring, the summer
> The childing autumn, angry winter, change
> Their wonted liveries; and the mazed world,
> By their increase, now knows not which is which.

And then from describing nature at war with herself, Shakespeare turns to the political tension of the day:

> And this same progeny of evils comes
> From our debate, from our dissension;
> We are their parents and original. (II. i. 93ff.)

Here, as in *King John* (V. vii. 113ff.), also of this period, Shakespeare warns that, if England divides herself, she will also destroy herself. When one thinks of the gathering political storm as Robert Cecil and Essex fought for the leadership of the Government, and of the still deep religious divisions, one is impressed by the acute relevance of the warning.

In 1601, in Parliament, the Queen faced an open challenge to her prerogative; and in the streets of London there had been the open threat to her power by the Essex rebels. In the last Shakespearian decade of her reign there were still the progresses and pageantry, the masques and the dances, but the glory of the high Elizabethan period was fading; the suffering, the doubts, the scepticism came more readily to the surface. Only eight years after her death, John Donne was writing

> And new Philosophy calls all in doubt,
> The Element of fire is quite put out;
> The Sun is lost, and th' earth, and no man's wit,
> Can well direct him where to look for it . . .
> 'Tis all in pieces, all coherence gone.[20]

It may perhaps be said that I have painted too sombre a picture of the late Elizabethan age. That is not my intention; but when one looks at Shakespeare's world in the theatre and out of doors, can one for long escape the harsh realities of the political and social scene? The analytical historian is primarily concerned with the nature of power, its use and abuse; political power, economic power, social power, the struggle to gain it and retain it. It is sometimes said that the ordinary man who comprised the texture of history was not involved in these things. I think that he was involved—just as he is in our own day—and the impact of political decision touched him closely. And when we turn again to the plays of Shakespeare, can we escape the feeling that the nature of political power—and the struggle for it—were very much in his mind? We think of *Richard II, Henry IV, Julius Caesar, Hamlet, Macbeth* and many more. Need we indeed remind ourselves that, in 1601, when the Earl of Essex was about to make his insane bid for power, one of his followers went down to the Globe Theatre to persuade the actors to put on Shake-

[20] John Donne, 'An Anatomy of the World', in *Collected Poems*, Nonesuch ed., p. 202.

speare's *Richard II*? The actors declined, saying that it was an old play which would attract only a small audience. But for the promise of forty shillings above their anticipated takings they agreed to put it on. The Queen herself read the bitter lesson intended for her, namely that monarchs can be deposed; and the Government took security measures to meet this threat. 'I am Richard II' the Queen declared bitterly to the historian Lambarde; 'Know ye not that?'[21] The point that I wish to make is that the Elizabethan London which Shakespeare knew was not the London of the 1560s or 1570s but of the 1590s. This is the decade when every unresolved political and constitutional problem which the Queen had postponed for so long cried aloud for solution. It is the time of renewed economic, political and social crises; and these crises are implicit and explicit in some of the greatest plays that Shakespeare wrote.

Of course, Shakespeare was a court poet and a court playwright; but what do we mean by the *court*? The social historian of Tudor England grows a little weary of the tinselled, splendrous prose of the glamorizers. Of course, the Elizabethan court was a glamorous place: with its masques and dances and amours; with its intrigues and spite and tedium. But it was also the centre of the Government of England: its monarchy, its politics and its Civil Service. In the days before constitutional government, it was the concentration of authority in one place. When Ralegh wrote:

> Say to the Court it glows
> And shines like rotten wood,[22]

he meant the whole fabric of government, not simply the elaborate charade of the courtiers. The story of Shakespeare's *Henry IV* is surely the story of a lust for power and of its bitter emptiness when gained:

> God knows, my son,
> By what by-paths and indirect crook'd ways
> I met this crown; and I myself know well
> How troublesome it sat upon my head. (*2 Hen. IV.* IV. v. 184ff.)

[21] J. Nichols, *The Progresses . . . of Queen Elizabeth*, 1823, iii, 552.
[22] W. Ralegh, 'The Lie'.

When the historian of Tudor England returns to Shakespeare his attention is arrested by the acutely memorable vision that Shakespeare gives us of the nature and problem of power in our day no less than his.

But if in these late Elizabethan years we detect in Shakespeare's plays, as we can detect a little earlier in Spenser's poetry, the growing crisis of the struggle for power, we have, too, plenty of examples of the gaiety of his genius, at its best. In the last two years of the century, at a time when the political skies were darkening, Shakespeare wrote *Much Ado About Nothing, As You Like It* and *Twelfth Night*. We remember, too, that the people who made up his audiences, although they lived dangerously, and all too often tragically, lived also at one of the great creative periods of English history and literature. For many of them, we must admit, life was drab, monotonous, discouraging for a great part of their lives. Sir Ifor Evans did well to remind us[23] of the long wintry nights of the Elizabethan people, whom we can only re-create in our imagination by considering the way of life in those parts of the world today scarcely touched by the amenities of Western civilization. 'Roughly one-third of the population', writes Dr. W. G. Hoskins of the mid-Tudor period, 'owned no property at all beyond the clothes they stood up in, the tools of their trade, and a few sticks of furniture: they lived at the level of Italian hill peasants today.'[24] In the course of the next hundred years things improved; but slowly, intermittently, unevenly and insecurely. Of these Elizabethan people our records tell us something, but all too little. But we do also see something of them in their robust country pleasures. They held life cheap; but when the harvest was good and the sun was shining, they played, and loved and danced and sang with a tough joy which would have astounded their descendants. It was that tough, almost irresponsible, confidence which carried them overseas to exploration, colonization, piracy, and war, at a time when their chances of return were often no more than one in two. They brought to their language a wondrous and rugged resilience which must be the envy of anyone who puts his pen to paper. We cannot attempt some social measure of the Elizabethan

[23] Cf. p. 23.
[24] W. G. Hoskins, *Provincial England*, 1963, p. 84.

people as a whole, for many of them are just names and some not even that. But the greatness of a nation lies in the greatness of its minority. There was an impressive minority of Elizabethan Englishmen prodigal of their skills, their energies and their lives; and they would bring distinction to any nation in any age. These were the Elizabethan people among whom Shakespeare lived, for whom he wrote his plays, whom he put into his plays, and who, in their turn, will walk the stage in many guises for as long as Shakespeare's name and work are remembered.

III

Shakespeare's Tragedies

WINIFRED NOWOTTNY

IN a lecture given in 1958, Kenneth Muir declared, "There is no such thing as Shakespearian Tragedy: there are only Shakespearian tragedies"[1]. Sharing this view, I shall not attempt much generalization, but consider, rather, what most notably makes each tragedy itself. Some exclusions must be made. *Titus Andronicus*, a repulsive play, may be left out without regret. As to *Troilus and Cressida*, one early text refers to it as a comedy; another, the Folio, calls it a tragedy; its form and tone have perplexed critics, and it is too problematical for inclusion here. *Timon of Athens* presents many anomalies; many critics think that parts of it were left in rough unfinished form; others, of whom I am one, have judged it to be only in part Shakespeare's. In passing over these three plays, I pass over, perhaps, interesting evidence of the effect upon Shakespeare of the tastes of his audiences, and the effect, too, of social conditions of the times. Moreover, *Troilus* is his most overtly philosophical play, and *Timon* the most critical of orthodox Elizabethan views of the organization of society. These cannot be passed over without loss, but their problematical character makes this necessary. It is for reasons of a different kind that I shall say little about *Othello*. It is that one of Shakespeare's great tragedies which presents fewest puzzles to critics; we need not ask what it is that makes it tragic, or effective, since these things are, I think, self-evident. To such questions about the other tragedies we cannot so readily give answers; I shall, then, mention *Othello* only in passing, that there may be the more time for considering the others. I shall, for the most part, take the tragedies in order of composition, so far as this is determinable,

[1] *Proceedings of the British Academy*, xliv (1958), p. 146.

but it is not my intention to attempt a scheme of Shakespeare's development; it is an undertaking hazardous enough already to attempt to come to terms with each play in turn in the space at my disposal.

I begin, then, with *Romeo and Juliet.*

A carping tone is sometimes taken towards this play. Sometimes it is said to be hardly tragic, since death comes about by a train of circumstances rather than from character; hardly about good and evil; in parts comic; much of it exuberant, much ecstatic. Even the love, some say, is often as extravagant in its expression as it is beautiful. Altogether, a young man's tragedy, and 'immature'.[2]

But Shakespeare was, to the best of our knowledge, in his thirties when he wrote it. And surely it is about young lovers not as they see themselves, but as a man of that age sees them—hence the comedy, the deliberate stress on the lovers' violent heedlessness, and the appreciation of the high style in which the young live. There is one moment in the play when the dangerous insolence of young men is perfectly caught—when Mercutio takes on Tybalt with 'Tybalt, you rat-catcher, will you walk?' The courting of danger, the quick sense of honour, and the swagger, are all there, and it is this moment in which the avalanche of the tragedy begins to move. The young fight and love and die in style—extravagantly, in hot blood, with folly and self-sacrifice and beautiful nonsense streaming from them in a non-stop glory. One has to have stopped being young to see how wonderful and dangerous this is.

Brought to the bar of criticism, the play will seem short of tragic only if we prescribe what a tragedy must be; for instance, that it must be about moral choice. As to its language, this will seem extravagant only if we demand that Romeo and Juliet should be less extravagant in feeling than they are, and that they should talk language such as men and women do use when they are not in love and not living in the sixteenth century. For, as Ringler points out, in his commentary on a sonnet in Sidney's *Astrophel and Stella*, 'The Elizabethans regularly indicate heightened emotion by exaggerated

[2] Cf. T. R. Henn, *The Harvest of Tragedy* (London, 1956), p. 73: 'immature tragedy, such as *Romeo and Juliet*'.

elaboration of conceit.'[3] Sidney, in order to express Stella's complete ascendency over him, uses this highly artificial conceit:

> When sorrow (using mine owne fier's might)
> Melts downe his lead into my boyling brest,
> Through that darke fornace to my hart opprest,
> There shines a joy from thee my only light;
>
> . . . .
>
> So strangely (alas) thy works in me prevaile,
> That in my woes for thee thou art my joy,
> And in my joyes for thee my only annoy.

The style of *Romeo and Juliet* is not more fanciful or artificial than this.

It might be objected that an elaborate style will do for a sonneteer but not for a dramatist. There is, however, very good reason why Romeo the lover, and Juliet, too, should talk like a sonneteer. The play was written in the heyday of the sonnet, and the language of the sonnet was the language of love. The kind of love Petrarch had celebrated was often regarded as an experience which lifted a man above himself, as an exaltation of the spirit so spectacular that only religious experience could compete with it for intensity. It would hardly have been possible for Shakespeare, writing about idealistic passion at a time when the sonnet vogue was at its height, to ignore the sonneteers' language for it.

And, indeed, the convention was very useful for his purposes. The fact that it was, at this time, so highly developed, made it possible for him to present the experience of his hero and heroine in language which could claim to be universal; it is the language of lovers in general, not of Romeo and Juliet in particular; they do not need individual characters in order to be able to speak as they do. None the less, they are sufficiently individualized, within the world of the play itself, by the fact that to be in their state of mind is to be in a world of one's own. Their world, to Mercutio, is absurd; it is a closed world to the Nurse; it is a world Capulet has no time for, and one of whose wilfulness the Friar disapproves. This contrast between the world of

[3] William A. Ringler, jun. (ed.), *The Poems of Sir Philip Sidney* (Oxford, 1962), p. 491.

lovers and the world of other people is itself a universal feature of the experience of being in love, and the plot of the play gives a dramatic heightening to this universal fact by placing this love in the midst of a feud between the lovers' families, so that it is the development of the feud, not the characters of the lovers, which destroys them. The plot itself makes a clear statement about the violent discrepancy between lovers and the world about them; to have individualized Romeo and Juliet would have blurred the clarity of this statement.

Shakespeare surmounts the difficulty of the second-hand character of this language by opening the play with a Romeo who talks at second hand himself, and later discovers the meaning of the language he has used. Romeo at first fancies himself in love with Rosaline and defines himself as a lover by a long tirade (I. i. 182–200), cast in the mould of that definition of love which comes at the climax of Petrarch's *Triumph of Love* (IV. 143–53); some of Petrarch's phrases recur, and the passages resemble one another in their use of a sustained barrage of contradictions declaring the contradictory nature of love. On seeing Juliet, he forswears his love for Rosaline:

> Did my heart love till now? forswear it, sight!
> For I ne'er saw true beauty till this night. (I. v. 54f.)

But his repudiation of his mistake is itself put in the conventional terms of a debate between heart and eye; the false object may have given place to the true one, but the language of love remains the same. So, when he speaks to Juliet for the first time, the dialogue of their encounter is cast in the sonnet form.

Shakespeare's debt to Petrarch and his imitators is not confined to formal and stylized passages; we can see it even at the height of the drama:

> Death, that hath suck'd the honey of thy breath,
> Hath had no power yet upon thy beauty:
> Thou art not conquer'd; beauty's ensign yet
> Is crimson in thy lips and in thy cheeks,
> And death's pale flag is not advanced there.
> (V. iii. 92ff.

This wonderful passage probably derives from the opening passage of Petrarch's *Triumph of Fame*. I quote the translation of the

Triumphs[4] by Henry Parker (1554):

> After that deathe had triumphed in that face
> ....
> Pale and horrible and proud for to se
> With hyr blacke baner awaye goeth she.

Romeo's words as he takes the fatal potion,

> Thou desperate pilot, now at once run on
> The dashing rocks thy sea-sick weary bark!
> (V. iii. 117f.)

contain a famous Petrarchanism, the storm-tossed bark as an image for the unhappy lover—an image which Shakespeare used in his own sonnet, *Let me not to the marriage of true minds*, where he says that love 'is the star to every wandering bark'.

The Petrarchan convention afforded such a variety of resources that it enabled Shakespeare, whilst avoiding monotony and disharmony alike, to maintain the pitch of lyrical utterance throughout a story which moves with such rapidity from one entranced moment to another—first sight, first exchange of words, first meeting in secret, first avowal, parting, reunion, marriage. And, of course, he does much to tie this language to immediate dramatic reality. For instance, the imagery of the lady as a source of light, so frequent in Petrarch, is used in the play in contexts where this imagery appears to be prompted by the immediate situation: Romeo meets Juliet by torchlight at the Capulets' feast, and 'she doth teach the torches to burn bright'; he sees a light at her window, and this suggests that 'It is the east, and Juliet is the sun'; when she appears, above him, she is not merely an angel, but an angel seen by one who falls back to look with 'white-upturned wondering eyes'. The nightingale, again, is traditional enough for lovers, but in the play Juliet will have it that the lark is the nightingale, and Romeo is content to agree, though it might mean his death if he were found. So Petrarchanism gives Shakespeare a repertoire of resources, which his own sense of fit language for particular situations enables him to treat selectively, and

[4] Henry Parker, Lord Morley, *The Triumphes of Petrarch*, ed. Stafford Henry, Earl of Iddesleigh, Roxburghe Club Publications, cxvii (London, 1887), p. 66.

to put in a convincing relation to the immediate context of the drama.

I have dwelt on the influence of this literary tradition not only to justify the language of the play but also to indicate where we may look if we need anything external to tell us where Shakespeare thought the tragedy of it really lies. In his own sonnets the great theme is that 'every thing that grows/Holds in perfection but a little moment'. 'This thought', he said in his sonnets, 'is as a death, which cannot choose/But weep to have that which it fears to lose' (*Sonnets*, 15, 64). His first really tragic drama is constructed as a series of brief perfections, each moment perfect because it is the first—until that one of them which is the last. The play needs no insight, in order to make it tragic, deeper than this, its chief insight; one so important to Shakespeare that it spills over into *A Midsummer Night's Dream*, where Lysander says that true love, exposed always to difference of blood, to war, death and sickness, is

> Swift as a shadow, short as any dream;
> Brief as the lightning in the collied night,

(we remember Juliet's 'Too like the lightning, which doth cease to be/ Ere one can say "It lightens" ')—

> That, in a spleen, unfolds both heaven and earth,
> And ere a man hath power to say "Behold!"
> The jaws of darkness do devour it up:
> So quick bright things come to confusion.
> (I. i. 144ff.)

To this Hermione replies, '. . . it is a customary cross'. It is, in short, a tragic aspect of the general human lot. It is no small part of the greatness of Shakespeare's first real tragedy, as of his later ones, that the tragedy lies essentially in the condition of man, not of particular men.

In later plays, the surface of the dialogue is less obviously encrusted with items transferred from a non-dramatic literature. But the endeavour to transfer the essence of other literature to the dramatic form is a feature of Shakespeare's work not confined to *Romeo and Juliet*. It is characteristic of his genius that he *was* able to devise a dramatic form for that view of life of which the Renaissance sonnet at its best had proved itself to be the ideal means of expression. This penetration into the very essence of another literature enabled Shakespeare throughout his career to realize the potential of the major conventions he inherited. *Romeo and Juliet*, if only because its indebtedness is so obvious, reminds us that Shakespeare drew strength from a literary heritage which was not England's alone. We may say of Shakespeare's tragedies that though their birthplace was England, their conception was in the literature of Greece and Rome and the European Renaissance.

Much of this came to him in translations, but he could read Italian, and, on a centenary occasion such as this, we may perhaps pause to acknowledge our probable debt to a young man who has had the unenviable fate of being both unidentified and frequently vilified, the W.H. of the *Sonnets*, who, Shakespeare himself tells us, 'advance[d]/As high as learning, my rude ignorance'; for whose delectation, presumably, Shakespeare incorporated in Sonnet 10 an allusion to Tasso's *Aminta* (Act I. sc. i: 'Ah, cangia/cangia, prego, consiglo') and in Sonnet 86 an allusion to Petrarch's *Triumph of Love* (III, 22: 'Quel si pensoso è Ullisse, affabile ombra'); for whom he entertained a kind of affection which might be better understood if treatises on Platonic love were as fashionable in our day as they were in his.

Some four years after *Romeo and Juliet*, Shakespeare wrote *Julius Caesar*. Some regard it as a play in which Shakespeare is not attempting much more than to bring historical events vividly to life; others regard it as a long step forward to the great tragedies, though not itself a great tragedy. It is perhaps for a number of reasons, tied together in a loose bundle, that it has figured as tragic rather than historical: a serious ethical issue is involved in a central deed, Brutus evinces conflict, he has lofty motives, the heavens declare the magnitude of the issue by a proliferation of portents, it ends in deaths, and, before the end is reached, we are induced to revalue the act that is central to the play, and the natures of those most concerned in that act have been set in a different light. Perhaps this last—the revaluing of the deed and of the people involved in it—is what does most to link this play to *Othello, Lear* and *Macbeth*, where the significance of what the hero does is seen too late, and to link it, too, in its emphasis on purposes gone astray, to *Hamlet*, where the Player King observes,

> Our wills and fates do so contrary run
> That our devices still are overthrown;
> Our thoughts are ours, their ends none of our own.
> (III. ii. 221 ff.)

It remains doubtful whether Shakespeare planned *Julius Caesar* so as to bring these elements into prominence, or whether, so to speak, he stumbled upon these things in the course of animating history. There is ambiguity in the play, and there has been much critical debate about Shakespeare's intentions. Is Brutus right to support freedom, or wrong to kill a great man, who is both his friend and, from the point of view of the public weal, defensible as a bulwark against disorder? Is Caesar great? R. A. Foakes, commenting on the ambiguity of the play, says that it presents

> problems that do not even arise in the discussion of many other plays by Shakespeare. The first concerns what the play is about and in what sense, if any, it has unity . . . to one critic the play remains simply a puzzle; to another it can only be understood in terms of *Antony and Cleopatra*, as the first part of a two-part play; to a third it is a tragedy with Brutus as a tragic hero. It has been seen as a play about tyranny, a play about Rome, a play about Brutus and as a play about Caesar and Caesarism; Caesar has been seen as the villain, and, so, perhaps more plausibly, has Brutus; both have also been seen as the hero.

Turning to themes and imagery for some light on these uncertainties, Foakes points out that 'the various themes are all used to suggest a full circle of events', and from this process of coming full circle he infers that 'the structural unity of *Julius Caesar* lies in the birth and completion of the rebellion', which he sees as 'a tale of frustration and disorder' which has no one hero.[5] H. S. Wilson, in his valuable study of the play, sees in this tale of a rebellion a significance and irony which he regards as fully tragic. He writes,

> *Julius Caesar* opens with the tribunes' foreboding of Caesar's mounting ambition and the contrasting irresponsibility of the plebeian crowd; it closes with the victory of the triumvirate over Brutus and Cassius. . . .

[5] R. A. Foakes, 'An Approach to *Julius Caesar*', *Shakespeare Quarterly*, v (1954), pp. 259, 260, 263, 270.

> In between these poles, we have the fall of Caesar and the moral tragedy of Brutus which it entails. . . . Brutus, in attempting to uphold the traditional republican ideals of Rome . . . actually delivers Rome into the power of the opportunist Antony and the coldly astute Octavius. . . . This is the design, then, of political events and their outcome which Shakespeare presents to us in the play. The human ideal of liberty is incompatible with the limits of human wisdom. . . . This fact is tragic for the noble-minded idealist like Brutus and for the great statesman like Caesar; and it is tragic for the state, for each member of it has his share of responsibility in the catastrophe. . .

and he finds in the play, seen from this point of view,

> a pervasive irony in the development of the motives and the action not unworthy to rank with the work of the supreme master of dramatic irony, Sophocles . . . It is the best classical tragedy in English.[6]

These two critics, then, arrive by different routes at the common conclusion that the play is structured as the tale of the rebellion, not as the tragedy of any one man. The case is well argued, and if, like Wilson, we also regard the play as clearly and impressively tragic, we must then agree that Shakespeare's second important tragedy, like his first, is not organized primarily to display the tragic character of a hero; his concerns are wider and more general than this. And, as in *Romeo and Juliet*, the plot, so far from being a mere pretext for the display of states of mind, is itself a powerful statement of processes to which the generality of men are exposed. And, even if we do not accord *Julius Caesar* as much admiration as Wilson does, we may yet agree that the overall effect of the play, especially in its strong coupling of convincing human episodes with a major deed that proves to be unmanageable by those concerned, is much closer to the tragedies to come than it is to the history plays.

It is unlike those to come in the austerity of its style. Though at its best it has that apparently easy eloquence already displayed in the later history plays, it brings home to us how much, in other tragedies, Shakespeare's effects depend on his achieving a language more evocative than this. When, however, we ask *why* the language

[6] Harold S. Wilson, *On the Design of Shakespearian Tragedy* [University of Toronto Department of English, Studies and Texts, 5] (Toronto, 1958 [repr.]), pp. 90–91, 96, 97.

of later tragedies is more moving, such answers as we can give are not stylistic only. So far as style is concerned, the deadly thrust of Volumnia, at the climax of her speech of persuasion to Coriolanus, is not so very different from the biting contempt which Cassius can command. Volumnia turns away from Coriolanus with the words,

> Come, let us go:
> This fellow had a Volscian to his mother;
> His wife is in Corioli and his child
> Like him by chance.
>
> (V. iii. 177ff.)

The difference in effect is due not so much to the style itself as to the situation in which it is used. Volumnia's speech, familiar as it is, is the climax of a profounder tragic irony which governs the whole action of *Coriolanus*. Yet, in the very fact of Shakespeare's using, for the climax of *Coriolanus*, language so sharply contrasted with the large rhetoric and the violence of many of its set speeches, we see his ability to turn back, at will, to a mode he had perfected at an earlier stage in his career.

Shakespeare's next tragedy was *Hamlet*. The sheer volume of criticism on this play attests the truth of one critic's remark that 'Hamlet is surely the most perplexing character in English drama'.[7] Yet at the same time it is, as Ridley says, 'the first of Shakespeare's great tragedies, the most famous tragedy of the English stage, one of the most famous of the world', and he goes on to say that it is with this play that 'one always feels, rightly or wrongly, that one is nearest to Shakespeare'.[8] Bradley goes even further. He writes:

> If . . . the question were put to us, which of Shakespeare's characters reveals most of his personality, the majority of those who consented to give an answer would answer 'Hamlet'. This impression may be fanciful, but it is difficult to think it wholly so. . . . Hamlet, we think, is the only character in Shakespeare who could possibly have composed his plays.[9]

[7] George Detmold, 'Hamlet's "All But Blunted Purpose"', *Shakespeare Association Bulletin*, xxiv (1949), p. 23.

[8] M. R. Ridley, *Shakespeare's Plays* (London, 1937), pp. 131, 134.

[9] A. C. Bradley, *Oxford Lectures on Poetry* (London, 1909), p. 355.

A. H. R. Fairchild, contrasting Lear with Hamlet, writes, 'Lear is a great personality. We admire him; pity him to the depths of our souls; but . . . we *love* Hamlet.'[10]

The world's verdict is that Hamlet is a fascinating personality despite (or because of?) the fact that we don't understand him, or don't agree on any one way of understanding him, or, to come to the heart of the matter, that we don't understand his attitude to the killing of Claudius, however well we seem to understand the way he looks at life generally. One reason for our having the illusion that the personality of Hamlet exists independently is that for much of the time he busies himself with matters other than the Ghost; the theme of delayed revenge allows Shakespeare to show Hamlet in a host of relationships and concerns.

But we cannot suppose that Shakespeare used the delayed revenge theme simply to hold the play together while he displayed the personality of the Prince; that he did not himself know, or care, what made Hamlet delay. This supposition is put out of court by the fact that Shakespeare *has* written into the play, and very didactically too, a comment on leaving things undone; in a passage in the play-within-the-play it is declared as a general truth, applicable to all men, that purposes dissipate themselves and come to nothing because of the very violence of feeling in which they are first embraced. The Player King observes:

> I do believe you think what now you speak;
> But what we do determine oft we break.
> Purpose is but the slave to memory,
> Of violent birth, but poor validity:
> . . . .
> What to ourselves in passion we propose,
> The passion ending, doth the purpose lose.
> The violence of either grief or joy
> Their own enactures with themselves destroy.
>
> (III. ii. 196ff.)

This point of view is reiterated by Claudius, in Act IV, scene vii (115ff.), when he is pressing Laertes to revenge quickly:

[10] A. H. R. Fairchild, *Shakespeare Quarterly*, xiv (1963), p. 69 [reviewing *The Living Shakespeare*, ed. Robert Gittings].

There lives within the very flame of love
A kind of wick or snuff that will abate it;
And nothing is at a like goodness still;
For goodness, growing to a plurisy,
Dies in his own too much: that we would do,
We should do when we would; for this 'would' changes
And hath abatements and delays as many
As there are tongues, are hands, are accidents;
And then this 'should' is like a spendthrift sigh,
That hurts by easing.

These passages are not accidental. They make the didacticism of general application.

This point of view is important in *Hamlet*, and in other plays as well. Macbeth, for instance, repeats the urgency of Claudius:

The flighty purpose never is o'ertook
Unless the deed go with it: from this moment
The very firstlings of my heart shall be
The firstlings of my hand. And even now,
To crown my thoughts with acts, be it thought and done:
The castle of Macduff I will surprise;
. . . .
This deed I'll do before this purpose cool.
(IV. I. 145ff.)

The closeness of these passages to one another is emphasized by the way in which both Macbeth and Claudius, on this topic, speak alike: Claudius with 'that we would do,/We should do when we would', Macbeth with 'If it were done when 'tis done, then 'twere well/It were done quickly' (I. vii. 1f.). And Claudius urges Laertes, as Macbeth urges himself, to proceed without delay, to allow no time for purpose to be aborted by the intervention of time and deflecting circumstance; purpose is thought of as coming to birth by thrusting with fast-shut eyes into a world that must not be suffered to touch it until the birth is safely accomplished. There is a comparable passage in *Troilus and Cressida*. Whereas for Claudius the image for self-frustrating feeling is the wick in the flame of love, for Agamemnon the image for the frustration of intention is the knot in the veins of the tree:

checks and disasters
Grow in the veins of actions highest rear'd,

As knots, by the conflux of meeting sap,
Infect the sound pine and divert his grain
. . . .
every action that hath gone before,
Whereof we have record, trial did draw
Bias and thwart, not answering the aim,
And that unbodied figure of the thought
That gave't surmised shape.

(I. iii. 5ff.)

Shakespeare sees it as one of the tragic conditions of living, that man is not in control of the processes of bringing purposes into being; his passions are the unstable driving-force, and time and accident frustrate both passion and deliberation. *Othello*, too, is relevant here, for that play is a terrible demonstration of what happens when a man freezes the flux of feeling at some chosen point and erects a monolithic purpose. Iago says to Othello, 'Your mind perhaps may change', and Othello replies,

Never, Iago. Like to the Pontic sea,
Whose icy current and compulsive course
Ne'er feels retiring ebb, but keeps due on
To the Propontic and the Hellespont,
Even so my bloody thoughts, with violent pace,
Shall ne'er look back, ne'er ebb to humble love,
Till that a capable and wide revenge
Swallow them up.

(III. iii. 453ff.)

In *Hamlet* itself we see more sides of the whole problem than we do in the other tragedies: we see Hamlet acting, disastrously, in passion, when he kills Polonius; we see him unable to kill when violence of feeling is wanting; we see him, at last, succeeding only because some power vaster than his own—Hamlet talks of 'a special providence' (V. ii. 231)—arranges everything.

These considerations are perhaps alien to some of our notions of Shakespeare's heroes as the makers of their own fates. Moreover, they raise the problem of how Shakespeare himself regarded moral action and choice. If, indeed, Shakespeare was expressing a serious view of these through several poetic dramas, a prose statement is likely to fall far short of the truth, but, attempting to put what I think was his view as best as I may, I suggest that Shakespeare thought of the conditions on which, as moral agents, we have to operate, as being baffling in the extreme. It is as though man, as a moral agent, were living in the wrong kind of universe; as though the incentives which drive men were intensely difficult to relate to their ideals of nobility and their expectations of others; it is almost as though Shakespeare saw man as struggling to do or to be something in a medium which is resistant to his attempts. 'What should such fellows as I do,' asks Hamlet, 'crawling between earth and heaven?' (III. i. 129.) The hero struggles to be noble or to succeed, in a context of laws which he does not understand. Man cannot understand himself or control his own future; there are fearful gulfs between what men think they are and what they find themselves doing; the deeds to which the tragic heroes address themselves become the focus of these mysteries and terrors.

Of all the tragic aspects of purpose and action which, as I think, haunted Shakespeare's mind, the one most prominent in *Hamlet* is the instability and dubiousness of feeling. This concerns Hamlet deeply from the beginning. His own intellectual allegiance is given to reason and to freedom from the drives of the emotions, as he tells us in the speech to Horatio immediately before the play-within-the-play: 'Give me that man/That is not passion's slave, and I will wear him. In my heart's core.' (III. ii. 76ff.) This ideal of nobility of mind is challenged by a situation in which a violent and passionate revenge is presented to Hamlet, by the ghost of his father, as the proper redress for murder. The discrepancy between the ideal to which Hamlet subscribes and the demands of the actual situation in which he finds himself could hardly be more acute. Hamlet does not so much fail to obey the moral imperative of the Ghost, as fail to resolve the conflict between that kind of moral imperative and his own conception of living nobly. This predicament comes home to the audience because the deed Hamlet is enjoined to do is itself morally ambiguous. The Elizabethan attitude to revenge was a divided and inconsistent one: honour demanded it, religion forbade it.[11] By choosing, for the central dilemma, an action whose moral

[11] Cf. Curtis Brown Watson, *Shakespeare and the Renaissance Concept of Honor* (Princeton, 1960), chap. 3, sect. 9, 'Revenge' [pp. 127–32]. On p. 127 he writes, 'The duality of Renaissance ethics is striking in any discussion of revenge . . . here the divided soul of the Renaissance most clearly reveals itself.'

status was uncertain, Shakespeare made it easy for the audience to continue to sympathize with a hero who accepts the obligation, but finds himself unable to commit the impassioned deed which would fulfil it.

Hamlet himself does not debate the ethics of revenge as such; Shakespeare does not present him as considering those facts about the death of purpose which Claudius expounds to Laertes, or as articulating a conflict between revenge and his own ideal of nobility. Though the elements of conflict, and the facts about violence, are included in the crowded canvas of this drama, they are present rather as a possible explanation of the delay than as articulated features of Hamlet's immediate consciousness of himself and his situation. There are, also, other facts of his situation, related to these, which are even more prominent in the whole composition, but, again, are not made explicit by Hamlet himself. What is prominent about this revenge is that it is a son's revenge for a father. If we attach importance, as I think we should, to the choice of *this* revenge situation (rather than, say, revenge for a brother or sister or wife), we may see in it a very significant comment on the concept of duty. Hamlet's dead father demands through his son a continuing hand in the structuring of events in the world from which he has been removed; he imposes on Hamlet the task of perpetuating the values of yesterday, of arranging the future in accordance with what has been transmitted to us from the past. Hamlet's experience of what it is like to accept this duty, and yet to be unable to perform it, is an epitome of the conflict of sonship; the conflict between respect for a father and concern for one's own status not as a son but as a man with a life to be lived. Hamlet cannot subordinate his manifold present to one overriding voice from the past. Because he cannot do this, he has a consuming sense of guilt and failure. This sense of guilt and failure, in a nature active and noble, is what gives the drama its tragic impact. That impact would be unimaginably weakened and trivialized if the sense of guilt and failure were objectively justified—if Hamlet really were a coward, a Jack o' dreams, an undutiful son. He is none of these. But his active and noble quality is displayed, not in revenging his father's death, but in the awareness he has of the living world. His responsiveness to it makes him the ideally compelling dramatic character, and this is established for the audience, from the very beginning, by his swiftness and accuracy in verbal response. The famous first words, when Claudius calls him cousin and son—'A little more than kin, and less than kind' (I. ii. 65)—set the pace. The same cast of mind appears again in his first conversation with Horatio. Horatio calls himself 'your poor servant ever' and Hamlet instantly corrects him: 'Sir, my good friend.' When Horatio calls himself a truant, Hamlet rejects this: 'I know you are no truant', showing again his insistence on the truth about people's attitudes and relationships. This same trait, at a deeper level, is shown (I. ii. 75f.) when the Queen asks why the loss of a father should 'seem so particular' with Hamlet, and he, replying, 'Seems, madam! nay, it is; I know not "seems",' brings home to us his determination to have things spoken of as they are, to make the outer man eloquent of the inner man.

Hamlet is soon to find himself in a situation where, one might think, it would be impossible to communicate his real self to others. But he is not silenced. His assumption of an antic disposition gives him licence to utter what he thinks fit. Shakespeare takes a further step to preserve the articulateness of Hamlet: he includes in his play characters who are not involved in the schemes of Claudius, so that Hamlet can move out of his antic disposition into a normal key, and so impress it upon the audience that his modes of communication with others are acts of choice; he is always in command of the verbal interchanges that take place, always knows how to manage the imparting of his meaning and his judgements, whatever the complexity of the relationship he is dealing with. In this sense there is indeed, as Bradley noted, an affinity between Hamlet and Shakespeare. Both are directors of dialogue, know what goes on, achieve communication. Hamlet's intelligence is shown as embracing all that goes on in the world about him, and as confronting, though he does not understand, all that goes on within him. His insistence on truth and awareness make him Shakespeare's best-loved character, and both the limits, and the reach, of that awareness make him a great image of the nobility of man. Thus the drama presents him—not marginally, but in the central area of the whole composition—as being pulled one way to duty, authority, the past, and the other way to his gifts for living, his creative nobility in the present. The beauty of Shakespeare's plot is that all these elements are shown in interaction. Allegiance to the past and concern with the present become, in terms of the play's episodes, something as immediate as Hamlet discussing the nature of drama with the players and then using them to find out where he and Claudius and the Ghost really stand—which provokes Claudius to spring the trap on Hamlet himself, and thus lays Claudius open to the counterwork of Providence. The crowded and variegated substance of *Hamlet* is a masterful image of the way in which all the forces in the situation combine in a living tissue of consequential events. That Shakespeare himself set a value on this aspect of his artistry is surely clear from Horatio's summary of the plot in the last scene (V. ii. 390ff.), introduced with the words, 'let me speak . . . How these things came about'. The plot then is not a frame for so many stills of Hamlet in soliloquy, nor a sop to the groundlings who looked for action. The plot shows how all the elements of the situation interact with one another; the holocaust at the end, which meets the astonished eyes of Fortinbras, is an image of the tragedy of a whole society.

In making *Hamlet* a study of the relations between the man of noble mind and the society about him, Shakespeare charged the old revenge convention with a weight of reflection and a multiplicity of significance which make the play a permanent challenge to criticism. And, here again, we see Shakespeare's power of handling, in the dramatic form, a theme on which much non-dramatic literature had already dwelt. Behind *Hamlet* lie the courtesy-books, the treatises on nobility, and the reflections on the nature of man, in which Renaissance prose literature was so prolific. The famous passage, 'What a piece of work is a man! how noble in reason! how infinite in faculty! . . .' (II. ii. 323f.), may owe much to Shakespeare's command of language, but it owes more to a tradition which goes back to Ficino and Pico della Mirandola,[12] and is continued in later Italian treatises of a Platonic cast. (There is reason to believe that the ideas of the *trattatisti* interested Shakespeare while he was writing his sonnets.)

[12] See *The Renaissance Philosophy of Man*, ed. Ernst Cassirer, Paul Oskar Kristeller and John Herman Randall, jun. (Chicago, 1948), pp. 216–22. J. Dover Wilson in *The Review of English Studies*, xxiii (1947), p. 78, suggested Pico as 'the source, direct or indirect, of Hamlet's speech on Man'; see also Frank M. Caldiero, *Notes and Queries*, cxcvi (1951), pp. 421–4.

Part of Shakespeare's strength is the massiveness of his themes, and the fact that they had been frequently pondered by other minds in the literature available to him. 'Shakespeare', says R. R. Bolgar in his book, *The Classical Heritage and its Beneficiaries,*

> is a product of a world that had learnt through imitation. He, Montaigne and Sir Thomas Browne may stand as our exemplars of the sort of mind that the Renaissance eventually produced. Just as the classical learning of the Middle Ages had crystallized in Dante, so the wider and more profound Humanism of the fifteenth and sixteenth centuries precipitated this new brilliance that stands at the threshold of our own epoch.[13]

The next tragedy, *Othello*, may serve to remind us how resistant Shakespeare's works are to any attempt to make out a tidy pattern of his development. *Othello*, in its study of revenge, has an obvious connexion with Shakespeare's reflections, in *Hamlet*, on feeling and action. Yet it looks forward even to *Coriolanus*, in choosing as hero a character 'little bless'd with the soft phrase of peace', a kind of character seen as peculiarly incapable of coming to terms with anything complex, peculiarly imperceptive—bound as it is to the service of its own adamant will which seeks to prevail in entirety against dishonour and rejection and even against its own affections. Between *Othello* and *Coriolanus* come *Lear* and *Macbeth*. *Lear* examines the father's role in society as *Hamlet* examined the son's. *Macbeth* probes again, but in a way far more horrifying, the errors in human calculations and designs.

Macbeth is about an outstandingly brave man who experiences fear to the full and fights back to the last. Every terror that might stand in the way of his taking his destiny in his own hands is confronted or overridden or simply borne; his will to shape his own life carries him through his fears of failure, discovery, execration by men, insecurity in his gains, loneliness, the invasions of the supernatural, his own horror at the initial deed and at himself, the want of meaning in life. It makes him such a monster of criminality that his deeds, as

[13] (Cambridge, 1954), p. 329. I should like to acknowledge here the generous help I have had from Dr. C. Fahy of the Italian Department of University College, London and Dr. M. A. Screech of the French Department, on those occasions when my immediate problems in Shakespeare studies made it necessary for me to ask guidance in their fields.

one of the characters in the play observes, 'strike Heaven on the face', and the end of this course of crime is that he dies like a baited bear. One question which the play provokes us to ask is a question about the meaning of such a life. A more immediate question springs, not from the course of the action, but from the quality of the experiences to which that action subjects the audience. The most striking thing about *Macbeth* is its power to engender terror; it can do this even when one reads it. No doubt the sensationalism of the play, and its thematic insistence on blood, darkness and confusion, together do much towards creating this effect, but I do not think that they are the main cause of the play's horrible grip on the imagination. Where the main cause may lie, is—to me—the most fascinating problem in attempting a criticism of the play. The poetry is the cause; if we ask what it is about the poetry that matters most, I can only suppose it is the prevalence in it of images which provide a language for that least articulate of emotions, panic. Panic, the nameless fear, finds its equivalent in this play in images of vastness apprehended by the lonely identity, as in:

> Now o'er the one half world
> Nature seems dead, and wicked dreams abuse
> The curtain'd sleep . . .
> . . . .
> and wither'd murder
> Alarum'd by his sentinel, the wolf,
> . . . .
> . . . . towards his design
> Moves like a ghost,
>
> (II. i. 49ff.)

or again in

> Light thickens; and the crow
> Makes wing to the rooky wood. . . . .
> . . . .
> Whiles night's black agents to their preys do rouse.
>
> (III. ii. 50ff.)

In both these passages—the one spoken before the murder of Duncan, the other before the murder of Banquo—horror lurks in the vast space over which the lonely eye seems to travel (over half of the world, over the darkening landscape); stirring in this emptiness is the one sinister figure (withered murder, the wolf, the ghost, the crow) which—and this is the root of horror—is an image for the speaker *himself*; the menace that seems to gather and thicken in the empty air is not anything he can keep at bay by steeling his nerve, because the sinister and terrible has, indeed, already invaded him; *he* is the horror which swells with menace. I do not know any other poetry which so successfully voices that sense of imminent invasion, of being swamped, which all of us inarticulately know in our own moments of black panic. One can see similar qualities in the famous passage about the blood on his hand:

> Will all great Neptune's ocean wash this blood
> Clean from my hand? No, this my hand will rather
> The multitudinous seas incarnadine. . .
> (II. ii. 60ff.)

and again in the passage where

> heaven's cherubim, horsed
> Upon the sightless couriers of the air
> Shall blow the horrid deed in every eye.
> (I. vii. 22ff.)

In these passages there is some vast, half-grasped otherness on the very point of reaching its goal, making its contact, sweeping over him—and in all of them, there is a subtle but terrible change of direction when the enormous, which is outside, or over there, or above, suddenly proves to be located *within* the man who is afraid, to be already stirring and burgeoning and pouring outwards, walking over the world or drowning the wind or making the green seas red. Shakespeare has found out a language for guilt and fear. It is a language which touches the verge of the incomprehensible, of nightmare or apocalypse or hallucination. It has to be a language of this kind, since it is the language that expresses the kind of fear we undergo when we see the bastions of our identity dissolving like smoke, so that we are exposed to the invasion of our personalities by what should stay distinct from them, and at the same time all that ought to stay hidden and controlled within us gets loose and rages at large. This language exposes the very roots of inarticulate horror;

that Shakespeare can invent a language even for this shows, as perhaps nothing else could, that his powers of creation are of a kind that must outstrip our powers of criticism.

It is very clear, in this tragedy, that Shakespeare is now aware of levels of experience that need symbols to express them. The symbols are not only in the poetry, but in the action. The porter of Macbeth's castle becomes the porter of hell-gate. There is an imaginative rightness in this to which it is presumptuous to try to tie any labels, but perhaps we might reflect that this is poetry in which man himself is seen as the porter of the gate against evil; the greatness of the play is that it is able to *say* that once the gate is unlocked, hell turns out to be inside in the castle, as well as outside with the witches on the heath. Banquo's ghost taking his place at the feast is a symbol of guilt—as well as a theatrical sensation. Macbeth descending the stairs from the murder, coming down to the stage to tell us about the horror of the deed which took place somewhere else, somewhere out of sight, speaks directly to us at that imaginative level where we understand that to violate one's own moral nature is to move into a plane of experience entirely different from that of ordinary men. The eloquence of symbols is now entirely at Shakespeare's command. Perhaps, then, it was inevitable that the end of *Macbeth*, which concerns the restoration of public order, and falls with a bump from the study of man's moral nature to the mere planning of suitable punishment and the extirpation of the criminal, should seem inadequate when it is compared with those parts of the play which have shown us what it was that Macbeth experienced when he took his courage in his hand and, armed with that alone, tried to make himself master of his own destiny.

Opinions differ on the question of whether *Macbeth* preceded or followed *Lear*, which is known to have been performed in December 1606. It seems best, in any case, to have discussed *Macbeth* before *Lear*, which, though again deeply concerned with good and evil, is immeasurably greater than *Macbeth*.

Lear is not concerned with a heroic effort to shape a course for one's life. It begins when Lear's active life is laid aside. It is concerned with what people expect, need, and get from others, and with what they choose to give or to deny. In the course of the play the hero's own concerns widen into a concern for the nature of society; this concern stands in a natural connexion with the kind of thing he finds he needs himself. The action opens with a question, from Lear, which many have thought arbitrary and childish: 'Which of you shall we say doth love us most?' In ordinary life, old people perhaps do not ask this question as directly as Lear does; in this sense the drama does not attempt naturalism. But because this is the fundamental question for all who are at the mercy of others, as the old and powerless are, the play is true to life in a dimension larger than that of mere naturalism.

The play is not concerned, either, with probing motives. It leaves them as an insoluble mystery, as Lear asks, simply (III. vi. 81f.), 'Is there any cause in nature that makes these hard hearts?'; no answer is given. It has often been observed how sharply the characters in the play divide into good and bad. No explanation is given for the savagery of Goneril, Regan and Cornwall, or the loyalty of Cordelia, Kent, Gloucester, Edgar, and the Fool. Yet, despite this, there is no play of Shakespeare's which makes us realize more keenly that nothing matters more than willingness or unwillingness to succour others, and no other play of his shows more clearly what a high price has to be paid for belonging to the side of those who believe in human kindness. Simple kindness costs lives. The most striking thing, then, about this tragedy is the intensity with which it focuses on the issue of good against evil, simplifying matters which in real life and indeed in Shakespeare's other tragedies are usually thought of as complex. Ridley has very clearly described the irreducible question which the play attacks:

> It is as though Shakespeare had proposed a challenge to himself. The question is not whether good is likely in this world to be physically and materially triumphant; that sort of triumph is . . . only in children's fairy tales. The question is something far more important than that; it is whether the good is indefeasibly *good*; not whether evil can 'conquer' it, which it doubtless can and often does, but whether it can *change* it, which would be the real and fatal conquest. In this play Shakespeare met his own challenge, and once for all answered it.

And, recognizing the starkness of this issue, Ridley also recognizes the difficulty of understanding the means by which Shakespeare involves us in it and impresses it upon us; he comments:

> The prodigious impact of the play upon our emotions is beyond question; and yet when one comes to examine it in detail one begins to wonder whence it derives this singular power.[14]

Lear is indeed particularly resistant to the kind of criticism it has been customary to apply to Shakespeare—to analysis of its characters and themes (which it defies by simplicity). In order to discern where the art of its creator lies, we have to look, instead, at the larger features of its structure. First, the plot. It is designed for universality: Gloucester's story runs parallel to Lear's, with only that kind of contrast which stresses the significance of the parallel, in that Gloucester, giving nothing away, has it taken from him, and his extreme of suffering is physical, whereas Lear, apart from his exposure to the elements, suffers most in heart and mind; these differences in their experience, while their treatment by their children is basically alike, serve to make up a total picture of the dependence of the old on the natures of their children, and of the sufferings they must endure. Again, the setting of the drama aims at universality. It is set in an almost timeless, a legendary England, with no locations in it except for the cliffs of Dover and a shadowy France—for the rest, the nameless heath, the nameless houses of the great, the nameless villages of poor Tom's wanderings. Almost all we know about the organization of the society in which it takes place is that people are divided into the haves and the have-nots, the powerful and the weak.

This striving for universality is carried even into the presentation of the hero. Lear has no tempter, as Othello and Macbeth have, no problem created by other people's histories, as Hamlet and Romeo have; he has only what comes out of his situation as an old man, defenceless because he has given his power away. This simplicity is even carried into the language of the play, which, except for Lear's Titanic defiance of the storm, is never stagey or obviously 'poetical', and almost always owes its tragic effect not so much to what is said as to who says it and when; the speeches owe almost everything to dramatic context.

Within all these self-denying ordinances which Shakespeare laid

[14] *Op. cit.*, pp. 172–3; 168.

down for himself, there are many processes of positive intensification—some of which, again, derive force from the basic situation and the plot. By virtue of these, Lear concentrates in his own person a number of symbolic functions and a number of moral claims on others: he is king, father, benefactor (to all his daughters in his own intention, and to two of them in fact), he is old, later he is helpless, victimized and mad. As his story develops, one aspect of his role interacts with another, and he is seen as a king without power, a father deprived of his children, an old man cast out, a benefactor to whom (so far as he knows, until almost the end) only ingratitude accrues. These sufferings lead him into other symbolic roles: the challenger of the justice of the gods, the outcast who achieves a new vision of society, the madman who knows the truth. When we reflect that *Timon of Athens* draws all its impetus from but a few of these roles and extends that impetus into a violence of language which has no parallel in *Lear*, we may see with new eyes both the restraint of *King Lear* and the much greater richness of its symbolism.

The language of the play, though it eschews what is theatrical or evidently poetical, achieves intensity by other means. Brilliantly, it uses what is already given on the stage, visible there, to work along with the words. Lear visibly is what his tragic situation is: old, outcast, crowned with weeds, carrying his dead child in his arms. Poor Tom is all the destitute in visible form. The hovel and the storm speak to us directly. Gloucester's blindness is before us. Kent in the stocks, Lear kneeling to his daughters, or restored and new-clothed in proper garments, say what the words need not repeat. The visual language of the play does much to maintain that continuous, unremitting impact which *Lear* has when it is performed. The evidence of cruelty and suffering, seen on-stage, asserts without verbal hyperbole the vast dimensions of the evil to which the characters of the play are exposed.

Within this large dimension there is one which might seem much smaller—a family quarrel. Everything starts there. Lear's obsession with his daughters' treatment of him, and the parallel case of Gloucester, ensure that all the wider concerns which enter the play keep on returning there—as when Lear sees Poor Tom, and exclaims, 'Hast thou given all to thy two daughters? And art thou come to this?' or when Gloucester is blinded, and says, 'All dark and comfortless. Where's my son Edmund?/Edmund, enkindle all the sparks of nature,/To quit this horrid act.' The indignation and pity of those who love Lear ensure that repeated emphasis is laid on such contrasts as Lear's defiance of the storm, and his pitiful frailty of body, and in a variety of ways the impiety of Goneril and Regan (the beginning of it all) is related on the one side to the great winds of suffering that howl through the world and on the other to the physical fragility of Lear. This network of relations is seen, for instance, in Gloucester's protest:

> The sea, with such a storm as his bare head
> In hell-black night endur'd, would have buoy'd up,
> And quench'd the stelled fires:
> Yet, poor old heart, he holp the heavens to rain.
> If wolves had at thy gate howl'd that stern time,
> Thou shouldst have said 'Good porter, turn the key,'
> All cruels else subscribed: but I shall see
> The winged vengeance overtake such children.
>
> (III. vii. 59ff.)

Cordelia's pity for Lear is in the same vein:

> Had you not been their father, these white flakes
> Had challenged pity of them. Was this a face
> To be opposed against the warring winds?
> To stand against the deep dread-bolted thunder?
> In the most terrible and nimble stroke
> Of quick, cross lightning? to watch—poor perdu!—
> With this thin helm? Mine enemy's dog,
> Though he had bit me, should have stood that night
> Against my fire; and wast thou fain, poor father,
> To hovel thee with swine, and rogues forlorn,
> In short and musty straw?
>
> (IV. vii. 30ff.)

So Lear himself, in the storm, decisively links together the elements, the gods, his daughters, and his own frailty:

> Nor rain, wind, thunder, fire, are my daughters:
> I tax not you, you elements, with unkindness;
> I never gave you kingdom, call'd you children,
> You owe me no subscription: then let fall
> Your horrible pleasure; here I stand, your slave,

A poor, infirm, weak, and despised old man:
But yet I call you servile ministers
That have with two pernicious daughters join'd
Your high engender'd battles 'gainst a head
So old and white as this.

(III. ii. 15ff.)

What is effective about this style is its remarkable consistency; Gloucester, Cordelia, and Lear all speak of the same complex of considerations. The vision of disruption of family which is one with all the cruelty of the world, and that cruelty experienced most by one frail old man, is the real centre of the powerful language of the play. Everyone adds to this core after his fashion, even the Fool: 'Good nuncle, in, and ask thy daughters' blessing: here's a night pities neither wise man nor fool' (III. ii. 12f.); even Poor Tom: 'Away! the foul fiend follows me! Through the sharp hawthorn blows the cold wind. Hum! Go to thy cold bed, and warm thee. . . . Who gives any thing to poor Tom? . . .Tom's a'cold. . . . Bless thee from whirlwinds. . . . Do poor Tom some charity, whom the foul fiend vexes'. (III. iv. 46ff.) In this respect the storm is crucial in the play, for it establishes the oneness of the daughters' cruelty, the elements' cruelty, and society's cruelty, and drives this home by use of the symbol of man's pitiful suffering flesh. To this symbol the other symbol of clothing is obviously connected. When Regan and Goneril are herding Lear into a corner in the quarrel about his retainers, he swings suddenly out into the larger dimension of the nature of need:

O, reason not the need: our basest beggars
Are in the poorest thing superfluous:
. . . .
Why, nature needs not what thou gorgeous wear'st,
Which scarcely keeps thee warm. But, for true need,—
You heavens, give me that patience, patience I need!
You see me here, you gods, a poor old man,
. . . .
If it be you that stir these daughters' hearts
Against their father . . . .
. . . . touch me with noble anger. . . .

(II. iv. 267ff.)

In the passages I have quoted, we can see the dramatist constructing a basic alphabet of symbols to express the unified vision at the heart of the play, and thereafter, in his use of this handful of symbols, in speech after speech, gaining in reiteration and intensity infinitely more than he could have got by variety, colour, grandiosity, or surprise. The symbols are such that they weld the family quarrel to all the ills of the world as they are suffered in the little world of man. The language, both visual and verbal, of the play swings us constantly from the great periphery of evil to the little human centre. It is impossible, when subjected to this amazingly unified language, to escape the realization of the infinite evil that can be experienced by finite man, and this indeed is the core from which comes the power which Shakespeare displays at the play's most moving moments, as in 'Let's see;/I feel this pin prick', or '. . . let this kiss/Repair those violent harms that my two sisters/Have in thy reverence made', or 'Pray you, undo this button: thank you, sir'. This sense of the infinite in the finite is present in *Macbeth*, too, but *Lear* is the greater play in seeing this with pity and fortitude rather than with nightmare terror.

I have left little room to pass comment on *Coriolanus* and *Antony and Cleopatra*. The first, much neglected, perhaps incurs its neglect by depending so much for its success on the existence of an audience responsive to the management of the set speech. It is a play of massive speeches, with an insensitive and rigid hero and a theme which appears to be political rather than universally human. It is often coldly regarded, which is strange, since it is a play which fully justifies the view that Shakespeare was capable of the most penetrating analysis of human attitudes. *Coriolanus* is a study of the rigidity of the military-heroic stance, and demonstrates with a masterly irony the path from superman to public enemy. Its tragic denouement, when Coriolanus, who has tried to be 'author of himself', is broken by his mother, is, so far as I myself am concerned, beyond question the most directly moving moment in Shakespeare's entire works. But I cannot hope, in the space left, to examine the art of this undervalued play.

There remains *Antony and Cleopatra*, like *Coriolanus* only in having a Roman as its hero, and an interest—but of how different a kind—in the nature of greatness.

Many years ago when I was a student at University College, London, Professor H. E. Butler, who held the chair of Latin, said to me, '*Antony and Cleopatra* is the greatest play in the world.' I was not then, and I am not now, in a position to make a comparative judgement of such a scope, but I thought then, as I think now, that it must be the greatest play in the world, since I cannot imagine how anything could go beyond it.

I have already declared that Shakespeare's tragedies do not lend themselves to the making of generalizations, and I have not attempted to draw, from consideration of the tragedies one by one, any scheme of Shakespeare's development. When we confront his greatness at its furthest reach, as we do in *Antony and Cleopatra*, we can see what it is that makes generalization and the tracing of development so extraordinarily difficult. Simply, the tragedies are too big for us. We cannot map them. If we look, for instance, at the things that are said about the poetry of *Antony and Cleopatra*, we find a host of critics testifying to a power which they acknowledge but do not profess to be able to explain. Munro, in his edition of Shakespeare, gives a summary of critical statements of this kind:

> In Alden's estimation, the language of the play has such power and beauty of phrasing that we are close to the limits of human speech. One of the greatest miracles of sound, remarks Edith Sitwell, that ever came into this world. The words, says Nicoll, possess a magic beyond the reach of any intellectual explanation.

Similarly, when he comes to his summary of critical pronouncements on Cleopatra, he remarks,

> Men write of her in superlatives. She has the attribute that she has attracted more descriptive cognomens than any other Shakespearian character, perhaps than any other female character in fiction or history,

and, offering his own comment on the construction of the play, he says that 'infinite variety is the intention'.[15]

And yet these comments, even though they reiterate the impression that the play outgoes criticism, may suggest to us some generalizations, not about Shakespeare's tragedies but about the nature of his

[15] *The London Shakespeare*, ed. John Munro (London, 1958), pp. 1209, 1214, 1213.

genius. It is a genius for language, above all; it was that which enabled him to embody any conception he entertained, however grandiose or subtle it might be. It is, moreover, a genius for putting himself in the position to be able to use his powers of language. With Shakespeare, the language that 'makes' the play depends in the first instance on his making the kind of play in which it is possible and proper to speak it. In the death-scene of Cleopatra the mingling of regality and simple humanity is breathtaking, not only in Cleopatra's own speeches, but in those made about her:

So, fare thee well.
Now boast thee, death, in thy possession lies
A lass unparallel'd. Downy windows, close!
And golden Phoebus never be beheld
Of eyes so royal! Your crown's awry;
I'll mend it, and then play.

(V. ii. 317ff.)

Or, again (V. ii. 328ff.):

First Guard. Charmian, is this well done?
Charmian. It is well done, and fitting for a princess
Descended of so many royal kings.
Ah, soldier!

What makes this possible is the initial choice of a tragic heroine who is an unqueenly queen, and a dramatic construction which first concentrates on enforcing the contrast between the splendour of Egypt and the unqueenliness of Cleopatra—so that at the last, when the death of Antony so transforms her that her baser elements are put away, the poetry can effect a fusion of the two images we have had of her throughout: the empress and the woman. Cleopatra is now indeed 'Royal Egypt', as Iras calls her, and at the same time

e'en a woman, and commanded
By such poor passion as the maid that milks
And does the meanest chares.

(IV. xiii. 70ff.)

Language such as this creates an imperishable image of the dignity of our common humanity, but we should not forget, when we give Shakespeare the credit for it, to give credit, too, to those who had gone before him and done something not unlike it. The substance of Charmian's speech over the body of Cleopatra is found in Plutarch. Cleopatra's dying words, 'Dost thou not see my baby at my breast,/That sucks the nurse asleep?' has a forerunner in the words of the pamphleteer Thomas Nashe—himself an example of the way in which, in Elizabethan popular literature, the ancient world was brought to bear on the concerns of everyday life. Nashe, in *Christ's Tears Over Jerusalem*, when he is castigating the vices and vanity of London, and adjuring people to correct themselves by thinking of death and corruption, illustrates his theme from ancient history: 'at thy breasts (as at *Cleopatras*), Aspisses shall be put out to nurse'.[16] Whether Shakespeare knew and recalled this passage in Nashe, or lighted on the idea anew for himself, hardly matters, but what matters very much is that he inherited a culture fed from diverse sources of vitality, and characterized by conviction of its importance, and confidence in manipulation. There is, after all, nothing quite so striking about *Antony and Cleopatra* (if we shade our eyes from its brilliance and think of its substance, form and values) as the fact that it rests on a medieval formula for tragedy, the fall of princes, and uses it to tell a Roman story, which expresses, incomparably, a Renaissance ideal of magnanimity—as reinterpreted by one capacious mind. Cleopatra may, as Munro remarks, be devoid of the 'king-becoming graces . . . justice, verity, temperance, stableness, bounty, perseverance, mercy, lowliness, devotion, patience, courage and fortitude'.[17] Of all these, save bounty and courage, Antony may be devoid, too. Yet they achieve and unforgettably assert, when they have lost everything except the right to die, something we all recognize as a sublime magnanimity, and an intensity, in the realization of their own natures and destinies, which shows us what, after all, is meant when we speak of the dignity of man.

This play, in its daring, its opulence and its sweep, may seem to stand apart from the other tragedies of Shakespeare. Yet there is one respect in which it develops from, and best expresses, the whole tragic energy of Shakespeare, namely, in its compassion—by which

[16] *The Works of Thomas Nashe,* ed. Ronald B. McKerrow (Oxford, 1958), vol. ii, p. 140; quoted by R. H. Case [*Arden* ed.].

[17] *Op. cit.*, p. 1214.

I mean that emotion we feel when we are made to experience, simultaneously, the suffering and the majesty of humanity. Compassion is the note of the epitaph spoken by Caesar:

> High events as these
> Strike those that make them; and their story is
> No less in pity than his glory which
> Brought them to be lamented.
>
> (V. ii. 363)

In Shakespeare's tragedies, the stature of the hero is shown most in his struggles with inevitable limitations and sufferings, and it is seen as being, at its highest, at once pitiful and astounding.

IV

Shakespeare's Treatment of Comedy

ARTHUR BROWN

If one examines the great mass of published work about Shakespeare's plays—a heart-breaking, nerve-wracking, and not altogether profitable business—one finds that generally speaking the comedies have received less attention than either the tragedies or the histories, and this despite the fact that they outnumber both these groups in the First Folio. In this respect it is of interest to notice that the pattern is very similar to that of the rest of Elizabethan drama. The records of plays produced in the Elizabethan theatres and of plays actually printed suggest that comedies outnumber tragedies during that period by about three to one; yet a consideration of the critical and scholarly work which has surrounded the plays, almost at times to the point of suffocation, indicates that, while the comedies have not been entirely neglected, they have, comparatively speaking, attracted less thorough examination than the tragedies. It will, I think, be useful to consider some of the reasons for this phenomenon before we look more closely at Shakespeare's treatment of comedy.

In the first place there is a fairly generally accepted belief that comedy does not require the kind of critical analysis that may be justified for other forms of drama; and, as an extension of this, that such critical analysis, when applied to comedy, will do more harm than good. Comedy, we feel, is by its very nature a light-hearted and delicate organism, at best easily misunderstood, at worst quickly destroyed when the critic gets to work on it. This attitude has been well summed up by John Russell Brown when he remarks: 'The boldest critic is apt to become modest when he writes of

Shakespeare's comedies; he is afraid of taking a joke or a fancy too seriously. While the tragedies and histories seem to invite his serious attention, the comedies evade it; on the point of expounding the "meaning" of a comedy, he hears a whisper, "But that's all one, our play is done". He may be sure that he has seen a "most rare vision", but he will prudently judge that it is "past the wit of man to say what dream it was". This modesty has often restricted criticism to praise and the expression of enjoyment.'[1] This is an attitude which undoubtedly receives some justification from certain of Shakespeare's contemporaries. Dekker, for example, can write in his dedication of *The Shoemakers' Holiday*, 'Take all in good worth that is well intended, for nothing is purposed but mirth, mirth lengthneth long life; which, with all other blessings I heartily wish you.' Only a slight extension of this point of view is needed to reach the position of Stopford Brooke on *As You Like It*: 'The solemn professor, the most solid moralist, will not be able to assert that Shakespeare wrote this play with a moral purpose, or from a special desire to teach mankind. He wrote it as he liked it, for his own delight.'[2] This was in 1905; yet only the other day, in a new book on Shakespeare, Peter Quennell still attacked as disturbing

> the efforts of critical admirers who, when they attempt a detailed analysis of the plays, attribute to them a kind of intellectual solidity and moral muscularity that the poet's innocent text can scarcely claim. Shakespeare's romantic comedies are neither serious criticisms of life or direct 'evaluations of experience'. Whatever a great artist produces must have some bearing on his attitude towards the world. But, as far as intention goes, the comedies are slight enough; Shakespeare set out to devise an entertainment, a dramatic fantasy or a poetic *capriccio*. His comedies have as little, and as much reference to the 'real world' as a picture of a courtly gathering painted by Watteau or a *fête champêtre* by Fragonard.[3]

This is a point of view with which, I confess, I have a good deal of sympathy, especially when I find a recent editor of *The Comedy of Errors* carefully drawing the attention of his readers to all the more serious speeches or 'notes of foreboding' which occur, as if to suggest

[1] John Russell Brown, 'The Interpretation of Shakespeare's Comedies: 1900–1953', *Shakespeare Survey*, 8 (1955), p. 1.

[2] Stopford Brooke, *On Ten Plays of Shakespeare* (1905), p. 155.

[3] Peter Quennell, *Shakespeare: The Poet and his Background* (1963), p. 168.

that we are about to move away from a merely comic world and settle down to something into which the critic can get his teeth—an expectation which, of course, is continually frustrated.[4] Yet in spite of my sympathy I should not agree that it is a point of view which entirely meets the case.

There seems to be a second reason, closely connected with the first, to account for critics having shied away from the comedies. Efforts have been made, and are still being made, in some quarters feverishly, to find more in the plays than entertainment, fine poetry, and lively characters; to isolate themes, to uncover meanings or what have been called 'Shakespeare's informing ideas'; in short, to do for the comedies what has been done for the tragedies and the histories. We are still reacting, I suppose, against the views expressed by Bridges in 1907,

> that Shakespeare should not be put into the hands of the young without the warning that the foolish things in his plays were written to please the foolish, the filthy for the filthy, and the brutal for the brutal; and that, if out of veneration for his genius we are led to admire or even tolerate such things, we may be thereby not conforming ourselves to him, but only degrading ourselves to the level of his audience, and learning contamination from those wretched beings who can never be forgiven their share in preventing the greatest poet and dramatist of the world from being the best artist.[5]

We should take a rather less jaundiced view nowadays of the Elizabethan audience, and as a result should pay a little more attention to the sheer entertainment value of Shakespeare's comedies, the level of which is clearly not as low as Bridges would have us believe. Nevertheless he, and others like him, have encouraged people to hunt for something more in the comedies, and the results have been at least unsatisfactory. True, it has been possible to point to a certain continuity of imagery, of ideas, even at times of themes, but few critics in this field have been bold enough to claim that they have thereby explained the comedies. I mention only two examples. John Russell Brown, in a very interesting book *Shakespeare and his Comedies*

[4] *The Comedy of Errors*, ed. by R. A. Foakes. (The Arden Shakespeare, 1962.)

[5] Robert Bridges, 'The Influence of the Audience on Shakespeare's Plays', Stratford Town edition of Shakespeare (1907), vol. x; reprinted in *Collected Essays*, i (1927), pp. 28–29.

(1957), attempted 'to define the "meaning", ideas, or themes of the comedies up to and including *Twelfth Night*', and isolated three main themes which he called 'the ideals of love's wealth, love's truth, and love's order'. Yet he added in his final chapter that these 'are combined and emphasized in many different ways, and alongside them, or rather, within them, many other themes are explored', and he seems to suggest at the very end of his book that we are still a long way from any agreement on what Shakespeare's comedies are about.[6] More recently, in a lecture to the British Academy in 1962, entitled 'Shakespeare's Comic Insight', Miss Mary Lascelles could end by saying, 'I fear that I have done little but ask questions, and, when I could not arrive at an answer, send others chasing after them' —which is at least a consoling thought for me!

Agreement on these matters is indeed hard to find, and this may well act as a discouragement to further hunting. How is one to interpret Malvolio? How did Shakespeare intend us to regard Shylock? Did he really intend Beatrice and Benedick to be the most important people in *Much Ado*? What are we to make of *All's Well That Ends Well*? Is it really designed so that the audience could relish 'a fine and delicate character' in an indelicate situation, as one eminent Shakespearian scholar has alleged?[7] These are not merely rhetorical questions; they have been asked over and over again, and the difficulty is that most of the answers seem to be different ones. Difficulties increase when we come to such plays as *Troilus and Cressida* and *Measure for Measure*. The former, as we know only too well, was described on the title-page of the Quarto as a History, while the Epistle to the Reader called it a Comedy, and the editors of the Folio put it between the Histories and the Tragedies. It has been called a comical satire, and one and the same critic spoke of it as a tragedy on one occasion and as a comedy two years later.[8] Professor Dover Wilson has spoken of *Measure for Measure* as 'written in much the same key as *Point Counter Point* and others of Mr. Aldous Huxley's novels. The hatred of sentimentalism and romance, the savage determination to tear aside all veils, to expose reality in its

[6] John Russell Brown, *Shakespeare and His Comedies* (1957), pp. 202–5.

[7] E. E. Stoll, *From Shakespeare to Joyce* (1944), p. 97.

[8] Cited by Kenneth Muir, '*Troilus and Cressida*', *Shakespeare Survey*, 8 (1955), p. 28.

crudity and hideousness, the self-laceration, weariness, discord, cynicism and disgust of our modern "literature of negation" all belonged to Shakespeare about 1603.'[9] Yet Professor Wilson Knight sees the central theme as 'Forgive us our debts as we forgive our debtors',[10] Professor R. W. Chambers as 'Judge not, for with what measure ye mete it shall be measured to you again.'[11] Roy Battenhouse sees a congruence between the Duke's actions and the Incarnation, Second Coming and Judgement of Our Lord.[12] Miss E. M. Pope suggests that the ideas of rulership and justice in the play exhibit Shakespeare as a man clarifying the ordinary Christian doctrine of the Renaissance in such matters.[13] One could hardly find a wider range of opinion, and if one proceeds to ask questions about the characters of the Duke, Angelo, and Isabella one is in very deep waters indeed. Small wonder that these plays have been dubbed 'Problem Comedies'; though a still small voice may sometimes be tempted to ask whether the problems are not rather in the minds of the critics than in the plays. A little more understanding of 'Shakespeare's World' might well work miracles in this direction!

The mention of Shakespeare's world brings me to the third major difficulty in the way of a full appreciation of the comedies—quite simply, their language. I must tread cautiously here, since Dr. Hulme deals elsewhere with the whole question of Shakespeare's language. I may, however, be allowed to make a few general remarks. Comedy is, by its very nature, a much more ephemeral thing, and much more closely bound to its own day and age, than tragedy. It would seem to follow, therefore, that comedy will be much more inclined to follow the current fashion in language than tragedy, just as it will tend to be dealing rather with current habits and ways of thinking than with the more important and eternal problems of mankind. The point does not need to be emphasized; there are examples from almost all periods of our literature. Now we have the *New English Dictionary* (which started life in University

[9] John Dover Wilson, *The Essential Shakespeare* (1932), p. 117.

[10] G. Wilson Knight, *The Wheel of Fire* (1930), ch. 4.

[11] R. W. Chambers, *Man's Unconquerable Mind* (1939), pp. 277–310.

[12] Roy Battenhouse, '*Measure for Measure* and the Christian Doctrine of Atonement', *P.M.L.A.*, lxi (1946), pp. 1029–59.

[13] E. M. Pope, 'The Renaissance Background of *Measure for Measure*', *Shakespeare Survey*, 2 (1949), pp. 66–82.

College, London, and now masquerades under the title of the *Oxford English Dictionary*), which can give us a great deal of help concerning Elizabethan usage; we have Dr. C. T. Onions's *Shakespeare Glossary*; we have Dr. Hilda Hulme's *The Language of Shakespeare*; we have Professor Helge Kökeritz's *Shakespeare's Pronunciation*, dealing with rhymes, spellings, puns and the like; we even have Mr. Eric Partridge's *Shakespeare's Bawdy*, which considers with enthusiasm one aspect of the problem I have in mind. All these are valuable in their various ways. What we do not have, and what we need very badly, is a Dictionary of Elizabethan English on the same lines as the *N.E.D.*, or perhaps more specifically, to begin with, a Dictionary of Elizabethan English as it was used in the plays. We should never forget that the Elizabethan theatre was a pretty closely knit world, centred for the most part in a London very much smaller than we can easily imagine, and I am sure that a detailed and scientific study of the language of this world, covering all the available plays of the period, would be of inestimable value in solving some of the knottier points of meaning in Shakespeare's comedies particularly. One has only to think how many cruces still exist in, say, *Love's Labour's Lost* which almost certainly depend on vocabulary alone, to realize how great the need is for something of this kind. We cannot hope to make much progress with the elucidation of the texts of many of the comedies until we know much more than we do now about the precise meanings Shakespeare gave to certain words; and one way of at least getting a little closer to these precise meanings will be to study the usages of his fellow dramatists at the Globe, the Blackfriars, and elsewhere.

This problem of language, and the even more tantalizing problem of possible references to current events and personalities, have helped to make the comedies a happy hunting-ground for the lunatic fringe of Shakespearian scholarship. Such problems have also succeeded in deterring saner students from inquiring too closely into their nature, lest they, too, should end by chasing will-o'-the-wisps into the slough of despond. One has only to mention the title of *Love's Labour's Lost* in some quarters to get the immediate response of 'School of Night', and any subsequent discussion of the play must give way to a discussion of the alleged private habits of Sir Walter

Ralegh, Christopher Marlowe, and George Chapman. I regret that I cannot be as confident as Dr. A. L. Rowse in linking *A Midsummer Night's Dream* with a particular noble wedding; in its chequered history the play has been linked with a good many such weddings, despite the fact that we are still waiting for incontrovertible evidence that it was ever written for any kind of wedding at all. Nor can I wax enthusiastic about the efforts to date the play by reference to Titania's remarkable speech about the bad English summer; such records as I have had the chance to examine suggest that the English summers in Shakespeare's days enjoyed the same high reputation as they do now, and whoever dates the plays by them must walk warily. The same principle applies elsewhere. That Shakespeare may have had a particular individual in mind when he gave us Malvolio seems to me to matter neither one jot nor one tittle; yet this, and many similar 'identifications', still litter the learned notes of our editions of Shakespeare, and seem to breed particularly freely in the comedies. I have no doubt that there were such references to current events and personages, and probably a good many more than we begin to suspect; comedy has at all times felt that such matters are its legitimate province, and in the closely-knit world of Elizabethan London we may reasonably expect to find a high proportion of private jokes. I would, however, insist on two points. The first is that no amount of searching in the historical material of the time is likely to elucidate these private jokes and contemporary references except by the most fortunate accidents and coincidences. The second is that the finest comedy does not depend for its existence on these private jokes and references, whether elucidated or not. It makes use of them; it absorbs them; but it makes out of them something entirely new and entirely different.

I have dealt so far very largely with the debit side of our studies of Shakespearian comedy, since I think it is important that we should understand reasonably clearly the difficulties that stand in the way of our appreciation of these plays. Let me try now to be a little more constructive. When Shakespeare turned to the writing of comedy, he had already served his apprenticeship in the drama in the composition of some of his earlier history plays. These early histories are not particularly good or particularly interesting, but they do show the young dramatist attempting to come to grips with his rather unwieldy material, and to mould it into dramatic form. When we turn to what is certainly one of his earliest comedies, if not the earliest, *The Comedy of Errors*, we are aware, I think, of a sudden mastery of this transmuting process. I do not pretend that it is an outstandingly brilliant play, yet more than one scholar has praised its clever adaptation of Roman comedy, and in its neatness of structure it has been referred to as the 'best plotted of Shakespeare's early comedies'.[14] There were several possibilities open to Shakespeare at this point in his career. The native English drama had developed its own forms of comedy from the Morality Plays through the Interludes, and that Shakespeare was aware of its traditions is clear enough from a study of his history plays. Models of classical comedy, in particular the plays of Plautus and Terence, were available to him both in the originals and in translations. John Lyly, writing in particular for the boy actors of St. Paul's Cathedral, had developed both the classical forms and a new, elegant, and polished kind of comedy of his own. It seems probable that Shakespeare was also aware of the various Italian adaptations of classical comedy in the sixteenth century. This is neither the time nor the place to go into a long discussion of these various possible models. What seems to me important is that the most recent editor of *The Comedy of Errors* has been able to devote almost ten pages of his introduction, quite justifiably, to a discussion of Shakespeare's sources for this play, and to show that, while the main source was undoubtedly the *Menaechmi* of Plautus, either in the original or in translation, Shakespeare must have been acquainted with a great many other versions and treatments of the same story.[15] Yet all these have been welded into a single whole in such a way that it is almost impossible to disentangle the separate strands. What is of interest, too, is the opinion of the classical scholar, J. A. K. Thomson, that

> while the structure of the play is Plautine, the superstructure is the work of a man who appears never to have looked at the Latin of Plautus at all.[16]

[14] T. M. Parrott, *Shakespearian Comedy* (1949), p. 105.
[15] R. A. Foakes in the Arden edition.
[16] J. A. K. Thomson, *Shakespeare and the Classics* (1952), p. 49.

In other words, at this still early stage in his career we find Shakespeare not only showing a considerable control over his material, but deliberately evolving for himself a new comic form.

It is perhaps fair to add a warning that some scholars have been ready to see a good deal more in the play than merely clever adaptation and construction; this may well be a reaction against Coleridge's description of it as a farce, 'distinguished from comedy by the license allowed, and even required, in the fable in order to produce strange and laughable situations'.[17] So we have those who would see an embryonic tragedy in the plight of the shipwrecked Egeon, those who would see a strain of weirdness and bewitchment in the subject of mistaken identity (as if this had not been a well-known subject for comedy for long enough), those who would point to the themes of personal and commercial relationships, of discord and final harmony, as foreshadowings of Shakespeare's preoccupation with such matters in his later and maturer works. There may well be an element of truth in these points of view, but I feel that it is doing a disservice to Shakespeare at this point in his career to stress them too much. It may be refreshing to hear this once-despised play spoken of as showing

> a playwright already beginning to generate, out of clashes between suffering and joy, disorder and order, appearance and reality, the peculiar character and strength that is found in his mature work,[18]

but perhaps we ought to be satisfied at this point with the excellence of his purely technical achievement.

Do we need to look for an incipient concern with cruelty or domestic strife in *The Taming of the Shrew*? We have no printed version of this play before the Folio of 1623, but the quarto of 1631 calls it 'a witty and pleasant comedy', a title which scarcely conjures up a vision of William Shakespeare sublimating in dramatic form his differences with Ann Hathaway. And for an age which found its amusement in part in watching the antics of the lunatics in Bedlam there would be little to take seriously in wife-beating. In any case, of course, the shrewish wife was quite literally in the Ark with Noah

[17] *Coleridge's Shakespearean Criticism*, ed. by T. M. Raysor (1930), i, 99.
[18] R. A. Foakes, *op. cit.*, p. li.

in the medieval cycles of mystery plays, and had a long and honourable history on the English stage. Need we take any more seriously 'A pleasant conceited comedy called *Love's Labour's Lost*', even if one of the frustrated scholar/lovers finds himself condemned to 'jest a twelvemonth in an hospital', and leaves the stage with

> Our wooing doth not end like an old play:
> Jack hath not Jill: these ladies' courtesy
> Might well have made our sport a comedy.
> (V. ii. 870ff.)

It is in this play that Shakespeare turns wholeheartedly to the models of John Lyly, the dramatist who introduced 'love and courtship not as mere incident but as a theme of comedy',[19] and who asserted:

> Our intent was at this time to move inward delight, not outward lightness, and to breed (if it might be) soft smiling, not loud laughing: knowing it to the wise to be as great pleasure to hear counsel mixed with wit, as to the foolish to have sport mingled with rudeness.[20]

But, just as *The Comedy of Errors* was Plautus with a difference, so *Love's Labour's Lost* is Lyly with a difference. The debt to Lyly has been studied in some detail by Professor Marco Mincoff; he points to the courtly setting and the courtly characters, the forsworn lovers, the contrapuntal structure, the static scenes of wit, the endless playing with words (the latter, incidentally, another traditional feature of the English stage, particularly prominent in the plays of John Heywood and other interlude writers). But, as Mincoff points out, in the first place Shakespeare

> gave to Lyly's airy nothings a local habitation and anchored them firmly to the earth. No mythology, no nymphs and goddesses, no mischievous Cupid, but only men and women, though, like most of Lyly's characters, courtiers and sovereigns. And in the second, the love that he depicts is no flirtatious game, no Petrarchistic sentimentalizing, though, to its cost, it assumes the outer forms of both, but a normal, healthy, human love with marriage in view. What Shakespeare retains from Lyly, and develops to the utmost, though with a certain satirical twist at the end, is the comedy of courtship—the capers of the men as they strut and preen themselves, the coquetry of the girls, who

[19] Marco Mincoff, 'Shakespeare and Lyly', *Shakespeare Survey*, 14 (1961), p. 16.
[20] John Lyly, *Sapho and Phao* (1584), 'The Prologue at the Blackfriars'.

> pretend they will not when they would, and plague their lovers and tyrranize over them as hard-heartedly as any Petrarchistic beauty.[21]

Notice once again that Shakespeare has taken over a ready-made formula, has tightened up the structure, has introduced rather more than a touch of realism, has given the formula an unexpected twist, and has produced something quite new. Once again I feel that it is Shakespeare the craftsman, Shakespeare the practical man of the theatre, who deserves our admiration here. And once again I suspect that Mincoff is pushing his conclusions a little too far when he sees in the satirical twist a possible indication that 'Shakespeare had suddenly lost patience with the very conventions he had been exploiting'.[22] I am conscious that I may be in danger of splitting hairs here, but I would suggest rather that Shakespeare was *enjoying* these conventions too much to lose patience with them: he was more concerned with seeing just how far he could take them.

I mentioned just now the introduction by Shakespeare of 'rather more than a touch of realism'. Words such as 'realism' or 'realistic' are dangerous enough in any form of literary criticism, and it may perhaps be better to speak rather of the 'anti-romantic' vein which appears in Shakespeare and a good many other Elizabethan writers of comedy. One of the best examples of what I mean occurs in Ben Jonson's *Bartholomew Fair* (V. iii–iv.), in which the puppets are used to present a version of the Hero-Leander story. We know of Jonson's respect and affection for classical material; yet here we find him turning the story completely upside-down, and coupling it with a quite savage attack on the ignorance of his audience. 'What do they know what Hellespont is?', he asks, and proceeds to revise the text to 'make it a little easie and modern for the times', giving it a contemporary setting so that the Hellespont now becomes the Thames, Leander the son of a dyer living about Puddle Wharf, and Hero a wench of the Bankside who is made to fall in love with Leander by the administration of a pint of sherry, supplied by a Cupid who now appears as an Elizabethan barman. We find Thomas Heywood doing the same kind of thing later when he allows the Clown of his play *Love's Mistress* (II. iii.) to retell the story of the Trojan War to a

[21] Mincoff, *op. cit.*, p. 19.
[22] *Ibid.*, p. 20.

group of awestruck yokels, in order to persuade them that they have been deceived by the versions put around by the poets. Menelaus becomes a farmer, 'who had a light wench to his wife call'd Hellen, that kept his sheep, whom Paris, one of Priam's mad lads, seeing and liking, ticeth over the brooke, and lies with her in despight of her husband's teeth'. Agamemnon becomes the high constable of the hundred, Ulysses 'a fair-spoken fellow' and the town clerk, and Ajax the local butcher, and the Trojan War is reduced to the status of an afternoon's bout with a pair of cudgels 'for a broken pate'. Shakespeare never wholeheartedly adopts this strain, although there is perhaps more of it in his plays than we realize. But we may see how skilfully and how tactfully he can adapt it for his own purposes in the version of the Pyramus-Thisbe story presented in *A Midsummer Night's Dream* by Bottom and his friends. There is none of Jonson's savagery, and although there is something akin to Heywood's unashamed fooling the whole business is much more an integral part of the play; one cannot, in fact, imagine the play without it. Again there is a considerable debt to Lyly and his 'comedy of courtship', but much more gentle fun-poking at the plight of the young lovers. There is Theseus, representing a love in which mind and body are given their full rights, standing a little apart from the action and commenting upon it wisely, magnanimously, sympathetically; in the end he is prepared to dismiss the whole business as a dream, and his opinion is borne out by the very title of the play. Puck's mocking 'Lord, what fools these mortals be', the Queen of the Fairies herself falling in love with a country yokel wearing an ass's head, Bottom's crew and their mangled, yet gloriously funny, version of Pyramus and Thisbe—it is difficult to believe that Shakespeare was doing anything but enjoy himself. The structure of the play is wellnigh perfect, the three strands of the lovers, the fairies, and the yokels being handled with a skill that is almost breathtaking. This time the ending *is* like that of an old play:

Jack shall have Jill,
Nought shall go ill,
The man shall have his mare again
And all shall be well.

(III. ii. 461ff.)

The comedy of courtship is presented both on a supernatural and on an earthly plane; we are not encouraged to accept Theseus's verdict on events, nor are we, on the other hand, encouraged to reject it. The events are presented to us through the eyes of all the interested parties, and we may please ourselves what we do or think about it all. Shakespeare's genius in this play appears not only in his craftsmanship, but in his ability to re-create various points of view convincingly, and to avoid showing undue favour to any one of them.

I have tried to emphasize so far two elements in Shakespeare's treatment of comedy which seem to me to be very near to the heart of the matter. One is his very great care for construction, and the other is his ability to involve himself sympathetically with a great variety of characters without identifying himself with any one of them. It would be possible to illustrate both these elements from any one of the comedies, and to show how Shakespeare was not afraid to experiment over and over again once he had become conscious of his mastery of the craft. Professor Harold Jenkins has shown how, for example, in *As You Like It* he had taken his comedy 'in one direction nearly as far as it could go', before he returned to an earlier method in *Twelfth Night*. 'Of comedy', says Jenkins, 'as of tragedy, action is the first essential; but *As You Like It* suggests that action is not . . . "the life of these things". It may be merely the foundation on which they are built. And *As You Like It* further shows that on a very flimsy foundation, if only you are skilful enough, a very elaborate structure may be poised. But the method has its dangers, and although Shakespeare's skill conceals these dangers from us, *Twelfth Night* . . . returns to a more orthodox scheme.'[23] This conjunction, in one man, of a real care for construction and an ability to hold himself aloof from his characters, is something rather rare in Elizabethan drama. Thomas Dekker, Thomas Heywood, and other writers of romantic plays for the popular stage, over and over again allow their plots to get out of hand. They know all the tricks of the trade—disguise, accident, coincidence, non-recognition, and so on—but they often show a lamentable lack of any control over them. If a play seemed to go down well, a second part could be written, with the same characters, and additional ones if necessary, going through all possible

[23] Harold Jenkins, '*As You Like It*', *Shakespeare Survey*, 8 (1955), 40–41.

permutations and combinations of their initial adventures. Jonson, Middleton, Marston and others were well aware of the dangers of this kind of thing; but they saw a different purpose in comedy, a satirical purpose, and put the emphasis on its corrective rather than on its entertaining values. As a result the construction of their plays was certainly tightened up; T. S. Eliot has even remarked of Jonson that he 'employs immense dramatic constructive skill', but goes on to add that 'it is not so much skill in plot as skill in doing without a plot'.[24] But we rarely have any doubts about where the sympathies of these dramatists lie, or what we are expected to feel when the play is ended. For better or for worse it was this kind of comedy which gained the ascendancy in the English theatre in the seventeenth century, and what has been called the 'Shakespearian synthesis' suffered a long eclipse.

I have said little enough about the great characters of Shakespeare's comedies—the Dogberrys, the Falstaffs, the Toby Belches, the Bottoms, and the rest of the immortal crew. I have done this deliberately, because I have felt that they are often in danger of attracting more attention to themselves than perhaps Shakespeare intended. It is probably true that the most common way of studying the comedies has been to study their characters, but it has led to grave distortions. Miss Ngaio Marsh, quitting for a time the world of detective fiction and speaking of her experiences in producing *Twelfth Night*, mentions with some asperity the kind of thing that she had seen in the past.

> There had been star Malvolios and star Violas. There had been remorseless emphasis on a single character or sometimes on a single scene. The words had been trapped in the net of a fantasticated style, lost in a welter of comic goings-on, coarsened by cleverness or stifled by being forced out of their native air. I had seen Andrew wither into a palsied eld, Malvolio as a red-nosed comic, and Feste, God save the mark, as bitter as coloquintida or the Fool in *Lear*. I had seen productions with choreographic trimmings and with constructivist backgrounds. I had, however, missed the production on ice skates.

12th Night

She summarizes very well what I have in mind when she speaks of certain modern producers

[24] T. S. Eliot, *Elizabethan Essays* (1934), p. 77.

> who in their search for a new treatment of an old comedy forget to examine the play as a whole, and fall into the stylistic error of seizing upon a single fashionable aspect of a subtle and delicate work, and forcing it up to a point of emphasis that quite destroys the balance of the production.[25]

Further, in our concentration upon the great comic characters, we tend to overlook how pervasive Shakespeare's comic spirit was. Does not Falstaff first appear in a serious history play, serving no doubt to entertain us, but also bringing home to us, much more forcibly than any amount of sermonizing could do, the enormity of the task facing the young Prince Hal in cutting himself free from the unquestionable attractions of this Lord of Misrule. *Lear* has its fool, *Macbeth* has its drunken porter, both of whom could be made to fit easily enough into plays of a very different kind. Possibly it was considerations of this nature which led Dr. Johnson to say:

> Shakespeare's plays are not in the rigorous and critical sense either tragedies or comedies, but compositions of a distinct kind; exhibiting the real state of sublunary nature, which partakes of good and evil, joy and sorrow, mingled with endless variety of proportion and innumerable modes of combination; and expressing the course of the world, in which the loss of one is the gain of another; in which, at the same time, the reveller is hasting to his wine, and the mourner burying his friend; in which the malignity of one is sometimes defeated by the frolick of another; and many mischiefs and many benefits are done and hindered without design.[26]

The ability to take a sufficiently broad view is most important in our study of Elizabethan and particularly Shakespearian comedy. We may study the construction of the plays with some considerable profit; we may study the characters, and if we are careful not to take them too much out of their context all may be well; we may gain a good deal by a more detailed study of their language. But we may do well to remind ourselves from time to time, for example, that Shakespeare was much closer to the Middle Ages than we are to him; they did not end suddenly on the day that Elizabeth ascended the throne, and many of their habits of mind persisted for at least another

[25] Ngaio Marsh, 'A note on a Production of *Twelfth Night*', *Shakespeare Survey*, 8 (1955), pp. 69–73.

[26] Samuel Johnson, Preface to his Edition of Shakespeare (1765), p. xiii.

hundred years. The medieval conception of comedy, 'Est autem comoedia poesis, exordium triste, laeto fine commutans', something which begins in trouble and ends in joy, comedy as understood by Chaucer and Dante, is also Shakespeare's conception in almost every instance; Sir Philip Sidney's conception, 'an imitation of the common errors of our life, which he representeth in the most ridiculous and scornful sort that may be, so that it is impossible that any beholder can be content to be such a one', is a very different thing, certainly touched upon by Shakespeare, but developed far more consistently by Jonson and his followers. Allegorical interpretation, another medieval notion, was certainly understood more clearly by the Elizabethans than by us, and it makes more sense of *Measure for Measure* than any other interpretation I know. They did not have to be told to look for it; it was a way of thinking which they took for granted. In these enlightened days we have no difficulty in appreciating the character of a Doll Tearsheet; but the Elizabethans would have had no difficulty either in appreciating the horrifying predicament of Isabella—chastity and honour were words which still had a lot of meaning for them. We should take into account the medieval ability to poke fun, to our way of thinking quite scandalously, at the things they took most seriously, and remember that the beginnings of English secular drama have been placed pretty firmly in the household and circle of St. Thomas More, where there was a catholicity of mind and a saving sanity of natural humour which even today shocks some readers of the saint's more learned works. There is a gulf between this kind of world and our own, where poking fun at serious things is looked upon as very daring, is accompnied by a snigger, and is sometimes graced with the term 'satire'. Alas for Ben Jonson! Yet even while we try to remind ourselves of these important matters we hear behind us the drunken carolling of Sir Toby, and his impatient 'Dost think, that because thou art virtuous, there shall be no more cakes and ale?' There is room in Shakespeare's world of comedy for all these things, without fear of discomfort or of overcrowding.

Let me conclude with one more quotation from John Russell Brown:

> Shakespeare seems to have found the affirmation of his ideals in comedy

particularly congenial to his creative mind. The comedies form the largest single group of his plays, and his writing in this mode is noticeably free and unconstrained. In comedy he found that he could be at once positive and unassertive, that he could work upon the imaginations of his audience without raising their purely intellectual responses, their prejudices and predispositions; and he could write without limiting his width of reference by explicit moralizing. Tragedy, with its focus on a single hero, its greater intensity and intellectual clarity, could offer other opportunities, but in his own kind of comedy Shakespeare was able to affirm his ideals while apprehending society and portraying the rich diversity which he found in human life. It was to a form of comedy that he returned when, at the end of his career, he wished to present his matured and comprehensive judgement on man in relationship with men, and on man under the Heavens.[27]

[27] *Shakespeare and His Comedies*, p. 205.

V

The Uses of History

GEOFFREY BULLOUGH

MY title is deliberately ambiguous, since I wish to consider both the values for human life which Shakespeare apparently wished to foster by writing about history, and also the dramatic use he made of historical themes for theatrical purposes.

Recent writers about Renaissance views of history[1] have found at least seven reasons given for studying the past, namely, (1) in an age of springing nationalism to celebrate and explore the past of one's own nation, (2) to explain the rise and fall of nations and empires, (3) to provide 'exempla' whereby to teach men, and especially rulers, how to behave, (4) to show the fickleness of Fortune and men's ability or inability to rise above it, (5) to suggest that like causes would produce like results in human affairs, (6) to advance the practical knowledge of strategy and tactics, fortifications, commerce, treaty-making, etc. Above all, however, the aim of historical study was (7) to help men to understand the divine laws governing stability and change in human societies, the relations between the individual, the family, and the State, the balance of rights and duties within an ordered commonwealth.

In England historical writing was mainly intended to support the Tudor régime, to prove the right and necessity of Henry VII's accession, to show all classes the evils of dissension and disobedience, and above all to warn subjects against unrest, rioting and civil war. Edward Hall put the general point of view at the beginning of his account of the bitter period between Richard II and Richard III:

[1] Cf. Lily B. Campbell, *Shakespeare's 'Histories': Mirrors of Elizabethan Policy*, San Marino, 1947, chs. v–viii; E. M. W. Tillyard, *Shakespeare's History Plays*, 1948, ch. ii.

> What mischiefe hath insurged in realmes by intestine devision, what depopulacion hath ensued in countries by civill discencion, what detestable murder hath been committed in citees by seperate faccions, and what calamitee hath ensued in famous regions by domestical discord & unnaturall controversy: Rome hath felt, Italy can testifie, Fraunce can bere witnes, Beame can tell, Scotlande maie write, Denmarke can shewe, and especially this noble realme of Englande can apparantly declare and make demonstracion. For who abhorreth not to expresse the heynous factes comitted in Rome, by the civill war betwene Julius Cesar and hardy Pompey by whose discorde the bright glory of the triumphant Rome was eclipsed & shadowed? . . . But what miserie, what murder, and what execrable plagues this famous region hath suffered by the devision and discencion of the renoumed houses of Lancastre and York, my witte cannot comprehende nor my toung declare nether yet my penne fully set furthe.[2]

The Anglican Church gave divine sanction to such warnings in its *Homilies* appointed to be read in churches, and particularly in the *Homily against Disobedience and Wilful Rebellion:*

> How horrible a sin against God and man rebellion is, cannot possibly be expressed according unto the greatness thereof. For he that nameth rebellion nameth not a singular or one only sin, as is theft, robbery, murder and such like; but he nameth the whole puddle and sink of all sins against God and man, against his prince, his country, his countrymen, his parents, his children, his kinsfolks, his friends, and against all men universally; all sins, I say, against God and all men heaped together nameth he that nameth rebellion.[3]

The miseries of war were great.

> But, when these mischiefs are wrought in rebellion by them that should be friends, by countrymen, by kinsmen, by those that should defend their country and their countrymen from such miseries, the misery is nothing so great as is the mischief and wickedness, when the subjects unnaturally do rebel against their prince, whose honour and life they should defend, though it were with the loss of their own lives: countrymen to disturb the public peace and quietness of their country, for defence of whose quietness they should spend their lives; the brother to seek and often to work the death of his brother, the son of the father to seek or procure the death of his sons . . . and so finally

[2] *Narrative and Dramatic Sources of Shakespeare*, ed. Geoffrey Bullough, iii (1960), p. 16.

[3] *Certain Sermons or Homilies*, 1864, pp. 609–10.

> to make their country, thus by their mischief weakened, ready to be a prey and spoil to all outward enemies that will invade it, to the utter and perpetual captivity, slavery, and destruction of all their countrymen, their children, their friends, their kinsfolks left alive, whom by their wicked rebellion they procure to be delivered into the hands of foreign enemies.[4]

Historical writings available to Shakespeare and sharing these ideas included such diverse works as the *Annals* of Robert Fabyan, the more consecutive *Chronicles* of Hall, Grafton, Holinshed and Stow; the polemical martyrology in John Foxe's Protestant *Actes and Monuments*; biographies such as Sir Thomas More's *Life of Richard III* and North's *Plutarch*; historical poems such as the ghostly 'complaints' in *The Mirror for Magistrates*, and the verse-chronicles of Warner's *Albions England* and Daniel's *Civil Wars*; historical plays such as the anonymous *Troublesome Raigne of King John* and *The Famous Victories of Henry the Fifth.*

Basically Shakespeare's Histories expressed the same assumptions as Hall, not because he thought them novel but because they were familiar to most of his audience. Shakespeare indeed founded his plays on political and moral commonplaces, and on stories which were well known at least in outline to an audience which enjoyed seeing its general expectations fulfilled, although some of the details would be new or forgotten. Undoubtedly he supported the Tudor régime, the monarchical ideal with its insistence on Divine Right and the mutual dependence and responsibilities of ruler, nobility, yeomen and populace. In an age when the nobility were ubiquitous in political and social life and their great houses lined the opposite bank of the Thames, spectators in Southwark would enjoy seeing the ancestors of living lords, or those who bore the same titles, playing their historic parts. For, as Hall wrote,

> what noble man liveth at this daie, or what gentleman of any auncient stocke or progeny is there whose lineage hath not been infested and plagued with this unnatural division?[5]

There is no record of what the ninth Earl of Northumberland, Essex's brother-in-law, thought when his ancestors were pilloried as

[4] *Ibid.*, pp. 614–15.
[5] *Narrative of Dramatic Sources of Shakespeare, ed. cit.*, vol. iii, p. 16.

traitors in *Henry IV*. Perhaps the 'wizard-earl' did not care, or did not dare to object, since his own father had been three times imprisoned in the Tower for disaffection and had killed himself or been murdered there. But another nobleman may have disliked the use of a family name and the change of 'Oldcastle' to 'Falstaff' may have been caused by a protest by Lord Cobham.

In his Histories, as in his other plays, Shakespeare gave the public what it wanted, and there is no reason to believe that he ever deviated from the political orthodoxy which at times he openly preached. But he was first and foremost a theatrical writer not a propagandist; hence the interest for us consists mainly in the specifically *dramatic* use he made of historical material and the light it throws on his development as a dramatist.

Although Shakespeare's English Histories did not follow the chronological sequence of reigns, they covered the whole sweep of ninety years from Richard II's reign to the end of Richard III's. (This is not counting *Henry VIII*, which touched the fifteen-forties.) This material was not all capable of the same dramatic treatment; so the dramatist was obliged to experiment, and in so doing to exercise his remarkable dexterity in play-making. If I spend some time on *Henry VI* it is because I believe that no other dramatist but Shakespeare could then have organized its particularly intransigent material so magisterially. The reign of Richard III was not so difficult, but that of Henry VI as given in Hall was a tangle of threads, with events at home and abroad following each other without obvious logic. For Hall the reign was one of unsteady decline, only unified by the Divine displeasure meted out in particular cases and in national disruption.

In answering this challenge Shakespeare developed a constructive skill which (as in *The Comedy of Errors* and *The Taming of the Shrew*) preceded the full flowering of his *poetic* genius. The first use of history was to make him select significant moments, to form patterns out of the chaos of the chroniclers' details, to search for parallels and contrasts in character and incident, to seek ways of suggesting that the bitter quarrels, the downfalls of selfish men and parties, were cosmically fated and fell into a design of poetic justice.

In *1 Henry VI* Shakespeare separates the war in France which went on through the greater part of the reign from most of the domestic events which were actually interspersed within it. He rightly ascribes the decay of England to private feuds among leaders and to the absence of central direction under a child king. An ominous note is sounded in the first scene, with Gloucester and Winchester at odds and Bedford trying to pacify them as he cries:

> Cease, cease these jars and rest your minds in peace! . . .
> Henry the Fifth, thy ghost I invocate:
> Prosper this realm, keep it from civil broils,
> Combat with adverse planets in the heavens!
>
> (I. i. 52ff.)

After the Messenger has ascribed the loss of French possessions (not really lost for another fourteen years) to 'want of men and money' caused by 'several factions' and 'disputing of your generals' we hear of Talbot's capture (actually in 1429) despite heroic resistance. The scene thus represents the turmoil and tension of a country left without firm leadership; and in I. iii. the conflict between the evil Winchester and the law-abiding Humphrey of Gloucester is continued.

Yet this play is not to be wholly gloomy. The war ebbs and flows, but victory tends more to the English than to the French. History is rearranged to show the English fortunes in a better light then Hall revealed. Maybe the play was written because Queen Elizabeth, though with 'lack of men and money' and much 'disputing of her generals', was helping Henry of Navarre to capture the throne of France. So Talbot returns and Joan of Arc is foiled, and though later Talbot and his son are slain, Joan is captured and we see that she has been in league with devils (which explains her limited success against godly Englishmen). So the English on the whole have the upper hand, and French Charles swears allegiance to English Henry. But the marriage arranged between Henry VI and Margaret of Anjou is an ill match, for it prevents the fulfilment of Henry V's ambitions and constitutes a victory for Winchester's cowardly peace party. In 1590–2 the play would be regarded as a warning against withdrawing from France. As York cries:

> Is all our travail turn'd to this effect?
> After the slaughter of so many peers,

So many captains, gentlemen and soldiers, . . .
Shall we at last conclude effeminate peace?
(V. iv. 102ff.)

Almost from the first Shakespeare is skilfully preparing us for the next two plays, showing Richard of York and Somerset plucking the rival roses of their factions in the Temple Garden (II. iv), Richard learning from the dying Mortimer of his claim to the throne (II. v), and Winchester ever plotting against the 'good Duke Humphrey'. Towards the end a new man arises when Suffolk takes a prominent part in arranging the royal marriage. He falls in love with Margaret ('O, wert thou for myself! . . .' V. iii. 186) and the play's last lines assert his aspiration:

Margaret shall now be queen, and rule the king;
But I will rule both her, the king, and realm.

The pattern which Shakespeare has elicited from the chronicles is one of ebb and flow in a complex of conflicts between England and France, York and Lancaster, warring groups and individuals. He obtains contrast and variety by frequently shifting the scene and the mood, by introducing parallels with a difference, as in the scenes before Orleans in Act V, when the capture of the witch Joan, who curses York, is followed by the capture of Margaret by Suffolk, and his love-talk ('Be not offended, nature's miracle', etc.)

In the next two parts of *Henry VI* Shakespeare develops this method of presentation in a better organized, more systematic way, for, as I have shown elsewhere,[6] 'he sees the course of the story here as a succession of waves as the tide of evil rises', a succession of waves in which self-seekers combine briefly for wicked ends, then separate, change partners, and make new combinations which in turn break up as new forces come in; the whole making a surging dynamic on-rush of dissension and violence.

Thus in Part II the mounting Suffolk joins with his enemy Winchester to pull down Duke Humphrey, while Somerset and Buckingham watch with fear and determination:

Somerset. If Gloucester be displaced, he'll be protector.
Bucking. Or thou or I, Somerset, will be protector,
Despite Duke Humphrey or the Cardinal.
(I. i. 172ff.)

[6] *Ibid.*, p. 99.

But even now Richard of York is preparing to mount in his turn, first in a scene asserting his claim (II. ii) which parallels that with Mortimer in Part I; then joining the Queen and Suffolk in planning the removal of Gloucester—but he has already set on Jack Cade to disturb the general peace. Suffolk is destroyed, Gloucester is murdered, the Cardinal dies horribly, and, though Jack Cade is put down, York arrives from Ireland in V. i to 'claim his right', and a brief campaign ends in his victory.

Part III continues this wavelike succession of intrigue, rise and fall. York, at the summit of his career and enthroned by the aid of Warwick when the play opens, is promised the succession, but three scenes later he is defeated, tormented, and cruelly killed. From this nadir of the Yorkist cause his sons Edward and Richard rise with Warwick's aid and wreak vengeance on Young Clifford. Henry VI, restored in Act I, is made prisoner in Act III. But now the victors fall out, as so often before in this trilogy. Another ill match, the marriage of Edward IV with Lady Elizabeth Grey, alienates Clarence, and makes Warwick turn to Queen Margaret. By the middle of Act IV Warwick is taking the crown from Edward's head and returns it to Henry, who makes Warwick and Clarence joint protectors, and incidentally promises a great future for young Richmond, who is brought to our notice because he is to overthrow Richard III later.

Henry's state of euphoria is rudely interrupted when he is seized by Edward and Richard of Gloucester (IV. viii). Soon Warwick is betrayed by his colleague Clarence, Margaret is defeated at Tewksbury, and Prince Edward is murdered by the three York brothers. Richard then dashes off.

Edward IV. Where's Richard gone?
Clar. To London, all in post; and, as I guess,
To make a bloody supper in the Tower.
Edward. He's sudden if a thing comes in his head.
(V. v. 83ff.)

Sudden Richard is. He murders the unhappy Henry VI and leaves the Yorkists triumphant.

The play is thus an impressive rearrangement of historical facts which depends largely on the skilful use of Reversal. But this is not all, for just as the other two parts ended with a new character arising who will dominate the next piece, so here Richard of York, who has already shown in III. ii his envy of his brother Edward and a 'cold premeditation to my purpose', resolves to 'make my heaven to dream upon the crown', and turns from general ill will to specific plotting. Note, too, that the inner springs of his misbehaviour are more fully portrayed than those of any previous historical figure, when in the great soliloquy of V. vi. 68 ff., he expresses the moral solitude due to his abnormal birth and body:

> I, that have neither pity, love, nor fear. . . .
> I have no brother, I am like no brother;
> And this word 'love', which greybeards call divine,
> Be resident in men like one another
> And not in me; I am myself alone.

The political and psychological foundations are thus laid for Shakespeare's next tragedy.

In *Richard III* the material made it inevitable for the dramatist to leave the chronicle of warring groups for an action derived from a single man. Shakespeare had not read Aristotle, and had no objection to writing the tragedy of a completely bad man whose behaviour could not arouse sympathetic pity and fear. He knew from Seneca and other plays medieval and modern that sheer wickedness could be made entertaining. The recipe for this treatment of the long catalogue of Richard's crimes given by More, Hall and Holinshed, is already laid down in *3 Henry VI*, III. iii. 124ff:

> Why, I can smile, and murder whiles I smile,
> And cry 'Content' to that which grieves my heart,
> And wet my cheeks with artifical tears,
> And frame my face to all occasions . . .
> I'll play the orator as well as Nestor,
> Deceive more slily than Ulysses could,
> And, like a Sinon, take another Troy.
> I can add colours to the chameleon,
> Change shapes with Proteus for advantages,
> And set the murderous Machiavel to school.

Indeed, in this play, though Shakespeare may have learned much from Marlowe, he 'set the murderous Machiavel to school' much more effectively than the latter did in *The Jew of Malta*, where Machiavel was brought on to the stage to speak a prologue.

What holds our attention in *Richard III* is the intensity of the man's self-obsession and the diversity of his devices, the sardonic humour and the intellectual ingenuity exercised by his ruthlessness in duping friends, enemies and the people. Even an erotic note, lacking in previous accounts, is invented, as with great oratorical power he wins over Anne, Prince Edward's widow, by the bier of Henry VI. Here the dramatist probably drew on Seneca's *Hercules Furens* where Lycus (unsuccessfully, however) woos Heracles' wife.

Mention of Seneca recalls other devices in this tetralogy by which chronicle material is given theatrical pattern, namely, the formal representation of the emotions and the use of the supernatural. The characters in *Henry VI* are only broadly sketched, but the incidents make occasion for passionate display, as in *2 Henry VI*, III. i and the scene of York's death in *3 Henry VI*, I. iv. Supernatural beings appear in Joan of Arc's scene with her demons in *1 Henry VI* and in the Duchess of Gloucester's conjuration in *2 Henry VI*, which is at once followed by a scene in which her husband proves his goodness by unmasking the false miracle of Simcox. Dreams, portents, premonitions and prophesies lend an atmosphere of Destiny throughout the three plays, from Bedford's forebodings after the death of Henry V to Henry VI's prophecy before his assassination.

In *Richard III* these Senecan features are intensified. Queen Margaret is reintroduced, contrary to historical fact, to rail on Gloucester in I. iii, and to prophesy woe. Later, in IV. iv, Margaret, Queen Elizabeth and Richard's mother, the Duchess of York, vie with each other in a great scene of stylized lament. Prophecies are recalled and fulfilled; the dreams of Clarence and Hastings prove well founded. Hastings ignores bad omens as he goes overconfident to his doom. In the fifth Act the Ghosts of those whom Richard has murdered rise to make contrary speeches to Richmond and the King, and reduce the usurper to desperation.

By such methods Shakespeare made the plays more than a dismal catalogue of greed and violence. He may be said to have learned his dramatic craft largely in the school of history. By the time he had finished his first tetralogy he knew how to organize the most refractory material into a dynamic, well-interrelated design, how to modulate through narrative, discussion, passionate utterance, irony, pathos, dialogue and soliloquy, how to keep his groups separate, to shift the focus between individuals. He had mastered the tragedy of poetic justice, but he had still to learn how to make a weak character interesting, for Henry VI is little more than a cipher, though occasionally pathetic in his suffering.

In *Richard II* the dramatist experimented in this difficult field. Maybe he already intended to write a second tetralogy to cover the years before Henry V's death, for there are links between this play and *Henry IV*, e.g. in prophecies of Henry's and Northumberland's futures and allusions to Prince Hal's wildness. But *Richard II* is best considered as a companion picture to *Richard III* and as an attempt at another kind of tragedy.

Most Renaissance political theorists preached passive obedience to all kings, even to cruel tyrants. But some distinguished between tyrants who had a right to rule and those who had usurped their position. The misrule of legitimate monarchs must be accepted as a visitation from God, but that of usurpers could perhaps be opposed and their removal by the people's leaders might be justified. Richard III, then, might be unseated by a nobleman of better title; Richard II, however, as a lawful king, certainly should not have been dethroned; so when Henry Bolingbroke, who, in III. iii. 196, declares, 'My gracious lord, I come but for mine own', suddenly announces in IV. i. 113, 'In God's name, I'll ascend the regal throne', he commits a crime against his king and a sin against God, as the Bishop of Carlisle at once protests, in an all-important speech which expounds Divine Right, breach of which causes the sadness of Henry IV's reign.

Now this situation and its consequences account for some of Shakespeare's difficulties in the characterization and tone in *Richard II*. Because Richard is wrongly dethroned and murdered the dramatist wishes him to have our sympathy in the last two acts. Yet since Henry IV was a good ruler, though a usurper (and he was also the loving father of Henry V), Bolingbroke must not seem just an ambitious plotter. So Bolingbroke is made more likeable in the first half of the piece and Richard in the second. But even in the first half Richard must not appear too bad for the transition to be made.

Hence Shakespeare makes little of previous actions which would have depreciated him and shown the rebels in a better light—for instance, his extravagance, the significance of the 'blank charters', the full story of his favourites and of Gloucester's murder (all features of that excellent play *Woodstock*).

Consequently the Mowbray-Bolingbroke duel, their banishment, and the nobles' support for Bolingbroke on his return are not fully explained. That is a dramatic fault, but it becomes possible to focus sympathy on the deserted king from the moment of Henry's landing.

To do this Shakespeare, following the example of Daniel in his recent *Civil Wars* poem (1595), develops the pathos of Richard's position. In doing so he makes him introspective, sensitive, morbid, the self-conscious analyst of his own situation, a poet, unfit for kingship but likeable as a man. The handling of historical material according to a preconceived notion thus leads Shakespeare to make the important step from the moralistic, judicial attitude towards the characters found in *Henry VI* and *Richard III* to an imaginative creation of the hero's inner life. At the same time the political difficulties inherent in the particular usurpation theme make his attitude to Henry and Richard ambivalent. His previous historical characters had been *either* good *or* bad; these two are both good *and* bad. As yet Shakespeare is not practised enough to make a unified portrait out of the ambiguities, the mixed nature of his human beings. In this tragedy of pity and reproof the good and the bad appear rather as alternate slices than fused together. But *Richard II* set Shakespeare on the way to his later histories and tragedies where he revealed the mingled natures of men and women in all their complexities of good and evil.

The switch from tragedy here to comedy in *Henry IV* and to comedy mixed with heroic drama in *Henry V* may have been assisted by Shakespeare's working over in *King John* of the earlier play, *The Troublesome Raigne*, in which already Faulconbridge, gay, cynical yet patriotic, stood for the true spirit of England, in contrast with the weak conscience-ridden John, who collapsed under papal threats, and in contrast, too, with the rebel lords who sinned against the spirit of England by bringing a French army into the country.

A mixture of serious history with genial humour could be put to better use, and Shakespeare had by now proved his mettle in comedy. Hence, when he came to continue the story of Bolingbroke, he developed hints which he found in another mixed play, *The Famous Victories of Henry V*, which may have had more historical scenes than are now extant and which dimly foreshadowed not only the Prince's pranks with Falstaff, the highway robbery, the recruiting, and the rejection of Falstaff in *Henry IV* but also the French wars and the wooing of Katharine in *Henry V*. Out of its trivial fooling Shakespeare evolved, with the more substantial aid of Holinshed and Hall, the pattern which weaves together the revolt of the Percies, the struggles of a remorseful Henry IV both to preserve his ill-gotten throne and to rule justly, the youthful exploits of Prince Hal, and the activities of Falstaff and his set. Since the reign fell into two somewhat similar parts, before the Battle of Shrewsbury and afterwards, two plays were almost inevitable. And this twofold division also suited the Hal material in the chronicles. The comic material was perhaps the more needed because the rebellions in this reign, though dangerous, were soon decisively put down and were not of intense moral significance—nor indeed was the second rebellion very interesting. Part II of *Henry IV* would show the utter downfall of the Percy faction, but after the death of Hotspur and the flight of Northumberland little remained except to tidy up minor figures, York, Mowbray, Hastings. The Falstaff material is all the more valuable therefore in Part II to remove the sense of anticlimax in the historical sections. In both plays the realistic scenes of town and country, tavern and highway, enrich the historical material so as to provide, not (as some critics have suggested) a complete survey of English life, but a picture of two extremes, a court burdened with cares and disorders, and an underworld of idle gaiety and disorder.

Critics have justly accused these plays of being repetitive. The political disorder in Part I is iterated in Part II in a narrower, meaner way. The prince's reform before Shrewsbury in Part I is followed by a relapse in Part II, indicated especially by the striking of the Lord Chief Justice, which is too shameful to be shown but is finally turned to the prince's advantage when, as Henry V, he praises his old enemy. The chronicle material did not suggest any character-development, and indeed Shakespeare at this time does not seem to have been interested in gradual changes of personality. Richard III had been all of a piece, consistent throughout; Richard II had been viewed from two angles; now Hal himself shows two sides of his nature. In Part I he turns to chivalry and duty from irregular life when he promises his father amendment and begs him to let his warlike deeds salve 'The long-grown wounds of my intemperance' (III. ii. 156). But in Part II he is still accused of 'headstrong riot', of wishing to usurp his father's place, as indeed he seems to have wished to do in fact (IV. v). So Hal does not develop; he undergoes two superficial conversions, the second one final because he becomes king. The conversions are the less real because in each play we are told that Hal is only playing the fool, learning his way about men, and biding his time. Psychologically this may be unsound, but theatrically it gives magnificent opportunities for different views of the prince and for a pervasive irony.

The question of the prince's filial truth and princely desert suggests to Shakespeare a way of relating several of the main characters in Part I by a thematic link which has often been discussed—namely the theme of Honour, which is diversely regarded by the King himself, Glendower, Hotspur, the prince and Falstaff. In this play the parallels and contrasts strike much more deeply than did the introduction in *Henry VI* of parallel scenes of supernatural and passionate display. Part II affords less opportunity for such a treatment. Instead we have illustrations of the truth enunciated by the king, 'Uneasy lies the head that wears the crown!' and, in the actions of the rebels, proof of Warwick's statement (which Adler in our own day has rediscovered) that men repeat the patterns of their previous lives:

> There is a history in all men's lives,
> Figuring the nature of the times deceased;
> The which observed, a man may prophesy,
> With a near aim, of the main chance of things
> As yet not come to life, which in their seeds
> And weak beginnings lie intreasured.
>
> (III. i. 80ff.)

—a notion borne out by the behaviour of Hal and Falstaff as well as that of Northumberland.

Another feature of the *Henry IV* plays Shakespeare seems to have evolved out of the need to link Falstaff to the main theme of disorder in the State. This is what one might call its 'Distanced Topicality'. Critics have often been surprised at Shakespeare's lack of those pointed references to particular events and themes of current gossip common in Jonson and Middleton. This makes the accurate dating of his plays and sonnets the more difficult. Nevertheless there seems often to be an implied reference to matters of current interest. I have already suggested that *1 Henry VI* may well have reflected the campaign in France, when Rouen was 'yielded up', not through treachery, 'but want of men and money' (I. i. 15–19). *The Merchant of Venice* may have been suggested not only by the Lopez affair but by a spate of writings about usury published in the nineties. Similarly the shameful, if comic, description by Falstaff in *1 Henry IV*, IV. ii, of how he 'misused the king's press damnably', and the recruiting scene in *2 Henry IV*, III. ii, are both comments on the sad state of the army and its amateur leaders and on obsolete methods of mustering the militia in the period after the Spanish Armada, when the country was still in danger of invasion. Shakespeare rarely introduced topical 'personalities' like his references to Queen Elizabeth in *A Midsummer Night's Dream*, to Essex in the Prologue to Act V of *Henry V*, and to the ancestry of James I in *Macbeth*. But he made use of fashionable literary cults, and touched lightly on problems of the time, and even a play so apparently remote in theme as *Coriolanus* doubtless gained in interest from the allusions to enclosures and to scarcity of corn, both burning questions in 1607 and 1608.

When Shakespeare had finished his English cycle he turned to Roman history, and especially to that part of it which concerned the death of the Republic and the coming of the Empire under Augustus. What special value had this for Shakespeare and how did it affect his dramatic art?

In treating of English history Shakespeare had chosen periods of discord and class dissension, of war either civil or foreign, in order to teach the lessons of concord and degree. He found Roman history equally instructive and capable of dramatic handling, and the Rome of Julius Caesar, Brutus and Antony especially attractive, because this was the end of the Republic caused by discord among world-famous leaders. Plutarch saw events from Pharsalia to Philippi as proof that Providence desired the establishment of a monarchy. Shakespeare makes as little of that as he does of republicanism. For him, as for Prince Edward in *Richard III*,

> That Julius Caesar was a famous man;
> Death makes no conquest of this conqueror;
> For now he lives in fame, though not in life.
> (III. i. 84ff.)

But Caesar's fame was equivocal. He was a great man, but historians differed about his merits. For some he was the conqueror who would have saved the State; for others he was an ambitious intriguer who would have destroyed its liberties. This is obvious even in Plutarch; for Lucan, Caesar was the enemy of liberty. The same ambiguity clung to Brutus's and Antony's reputations; for Brutus was a good republican who yet slew his friend and benefactor, and was placed by Dante with Judas and Cassius in the very jaws of Satan, and Antony, the noble avenger of Julius, was yet licentious, unjust and cruel, and degenerated into the minion of Cleopatra.

Shakespeare's reading of Plutarch in the period during and after the fall of Essex fostered in him a suspicion of politicians, his realization that even heroes had their weaknesses. Whereas in the English histories he had to preserve the traditional attitudes of the Tudor apologists, in approaching Roman history he was freed from this limitation; he could treat the characters more realistically and with greater detachment.

Moreover, the biographical method of Plutarch with his insistence on the significance of small details brought new opportunities to the dramatist, who after reading the three lives of Caesar, Brutus and Antony saw Caesar's end and its consequences as the result of an interplay between their personalities and the groups to which they belonged. Hence his play *Julius Caesar* has not one hero but three, each of whom is 'a power girt round with weakness'. Caesar's legend is so potent that he remains awesome even though he is depicted as overwhelmingly self-confident, pompous, uxorious and liable to the falling sickness; the legend indeed is more than the man, and Shakespeare points out the discrepancy between them. Brutus, most fully treated because he is the prime agent in the action, and the character Shakespeare admires most, falls victim to his own idealism, and to his trustful ignorance of the natures of his fellow conspirators. To emphasize this, Shakespeare ignores actions ascribed to Caesar by Plutarch which would have given force to Cassius's unsupported complaints against the dictator—his enmity to the optimates, his taking of property to divide among his veterans, his seizure of temple treasure. Instead Shakespeare makes Brutus determine on Caesar's death while admitting that he has as yet done no wrong:

> It must be by his death: and, for my part,
> I know no personal cause to spurn at him,
> But for the general. He would be crowned:

[Yet we have only the envious Casca's word for it.]

> How that might change his nature, there's the question . . .

[It *is* a question, no certainty.]

> The abuse of greatness is when it disjoins
> Remorse from power: and, to speak truth of Caesar,
> I have not known when his affections swayed
> More than his reason.
>
> (II. i. 10ff.)

But Caesar *may* become a tyrant, 'Then, lest he may, prevent.' So Caesar is killed on a presupposition; surely no good reason for assassination. And Brutus goes on to maim his cause by a series of misjudgements—of the conspirators' motives, of Antony's oratorical powers, of his own ability as a general.

The process of scaling down the giant figures of legend continues when we are shown the contempt of Antony and Octavius for Lepidus, and the easy way in which they each accept the proscription of their friends and relatives (IV. i). Similarly the quarrel scene which soon follows between Brutus and Cassius (IV. iii) shows sordid motives and suspicions endangering their relationship under stress. Their friendship, however, rallies, because it is soon to be all that is left of their tainted enterprise as they go down to death.

Thus Shakespeare, who in *Henry V* had gladly seized the opportunity to portray a hero-king who was master of his fate and equal to his patriotic task, has approached Roman history with a more critical eye, and created out of Plutarch a cool synthesis, appraising objectively a group of men, fatally interlocked, who were not equal to the world-shaking events they brought to pass. With *Julius Caesar*, one feels, Shakespeare was on the way towards the denigration of heroic and romantic myth which exposed the weaknesses of Greeks and Trojans alike in *Troilus and Cressida*.

We may be glad that, perhaps for political reasons, Shakespeare did not write *Antony and Cleopatra* at once in that anti-heroic mood. By 1607 he had lived through *Hamlet, Othello, Macbeth* and *Lear*. He came back to his sequel with these imaginative experiences assimilated, and able to conceive the tragedy of Antony and Cleopatra not as the chill moral and sentimental spectacle seen by the Countess of Pembroke and other classicists in their versions, but as a passionate conflict between duty and pleasure set forth through the Rome-Egypt antithesis, and the whole action was seen in poetic terms never previously achieved perhaps since *Romeo and Juliet*. Shakespeare's imagination had always bloomed at the thought of consuming love. Now his middle-aged eroticism has its final fling in portraying the fatal thraldom of his middle-aged hero.

How far the plot and characters derived from Plutarch it is not difficult to see. Less worthy traits of Antony and Cleopatra are ignored or glossed over—his cruelty in war and orgies in peace, her overriding ambition and mercenary nature. His shameful weakness over the Parthian campaign is omitted, and her perverse cruelty (for instance, testing deadly poisons on slaves to find which were least painful). Shakespeare has determined to dignify the pair, nay, to deify them. Undoubtedly he was strongly affected by the description of Cleopatra on the River Cydnus which he adopted so closely in II. ii. 196ff.;

> she disdained to set forward otherwise, but to take her barge in the river of Cydnus, the poope whereof was of gold, the sailes of purple, and the owers of silver, which kept stroke in rowing after the sounde of the musicke of flutes, howboyes, citherns, violls, and such other instruments as they played upon in the barge. And now for the person of her selfe: she was layed under a pavillion of cloth of gold of tissue, apparelled and attired like the goddesse Venus, commonly drawen in picture: and hard by her, on either hand of her, pretie faire boyes apparelled as painters doe set forth god Cupide, with little fannes in

> their hands, with the which they fanned wind upon her. Her ladies and gentlewomen also, the fairest of them were apparelled like the nymphes Nereides (which are the mermaides of the waters) and like the Graces, some stearing the helme, others tending the tackle and ropes of the barge, out of the which there came a wonderfull passing sweet savor of perfumes, that perfumed the wharfes side, pestered with innumerable multitudes of people . . . and there went a rumor in the peoples mouthes, that the goddesse Venus was come to play with the god Bacchus, for the generall good of all Asia.[7]

Their lives in the play at times *are* those of Venus and Bacchus; at others they behave with the extravagance of amoral idlers; all this in accordance with Plutarch's brilliant anecdotes which illustrate their daily life together, and the charm and intelligence which Cleopatra applied to her capricious spells. Note, however, that Shakespeare omits details in Plutarch which suggest a riotous vulgarity, e.g.

> And sometime also, when he would goe up and downe the citie disguised like a slave in the night, and would peere into poore mens windowes and their shops, and scold and brawle with them within the house: Cleopatra would be also in a chamber maide array, and amble up and downe the streets with him, so that oftentimes Antonius bare away both mockes and blowes.

From the first moment, as Professor Wilson Knight and others have shown, the dramatist's grasp of his theme is expressed through the imagery; imagery connoting transformation, unbridled appetite and dissolution. So Philo speaks (I. ii) of 'this dotage of our general', Mars is become the devotee of a 'tawny front', 'the triple pillar of the world is transformed, Into a strumpet's fool'. The hyperboles of Antony ('There's beggary in the love that can be reckoned') are set over against Cleopatra's taunts and reminders of his duty, which he rejects, calling dissolution upon Rome ('Let Rome in Tiber melt', 'Kingdoms are clay', etc., I. i. 33, 35), ascribing baseness to things of honour, nobility only to his heedless passion. These opening paradoxes are continued throughout the play, as 'witchcraft joins with beauty, lust with both'. Cleopatra 'makes defect perfection', and

[7] North's translation of Plutarch's *Lives* ('Life of Antonius'). See M. W. MacCallum, *Shakespeare's Roman Plays*, 1910, p. 311.

'vilest things become themselves in her'. Yet the movement of decay continues until 'the noble ruin of her magic, Antony' sees himself as like the vanishing cloud-forms, 'black vesper's pageants' when

> That which is now a horse, even with a thought
> The rack dislimns, and makes it indistinct,
> As water is in water . . .
> My good knave Eros, now thy captain is
> Even such a body. Here I am Antony;
> Yet cannot hold this visible shape, my knave.
> (IV. xiv. 9ff.)

After his death the movement for Cleopatra veers upwards again till finally she is transformed to fire and air and dies surrounded by similar images of dissolving ('If thus thou vanishest, thou tell'st the world/ It is not worth leave-taking', 'Dissolve, thick cloud, and rain'). So in this play the general outline of plot and the vicissitudes of the main characters are reinforced by images which emerge from their ethical and emotional implications. Recurrent images had been a feature of previous Histories, but never before had so much use been made of thematic metaphor to reconcile the violent antitheses of a whole play.

In both of his great love tragedies Shakespeare's poetic opulence is used not only to enforce the scenic opportunities afforded by story and character but also to rise above them. In *Romeo and Juliet* the poetry of love and foreboding serves to conceal the accidental nature of the dénouement and to make the lovers' deaths seem inevitable. In *Antony and Cleopatra* the poetry makes us suspend our ethical standards and accept and rejoice in behaviour which sets law, duty, morality at defiance, as we share in a fever and a passion which are not only of the flesh but of the spirit.

The appeal is from sober reason and judgement to our fellow feeling, our participation in natural passions and appetites which are good in themselves and so powerful that most of us have had both bliss and bane from them. By wit and eloquence which rise above but do not ignore the ways of ordinary lovers, Shakespeare refines and intensifies the Antony-Cleopatra relationship and makes it enviable as well as reprehensible, until finally we regard their deaths as both morally right and artistically suited to a passion which so enlarges the sphere of our emotional experience. In *Antony and Cleopatra* the ethical uses of history are for once transcended, and Shakespeare has at last written an historical tragedy in which the whole movement (as in *Lear* and *Othello*) is a poetic unity in conception and execution.

VI

How the Characters Talk

JAMES SUTHERLAND

WHEN a play is three and half centuries old some of the effect that it originally had is almost bound to be lost. Manners and customs and fashions and attitudes may have changed completely or become unfamiliar, contemporary allusions may have to be disinterred for us by erudite editors, and in one way or another the possibility of misunderstanding or missing what was once abundantly and immediately clear to a contemporary audience is considerably increased. And since a play is a play—a form of literature in which everything, except a few stage directions, comes to us through the speech of the characters—the most serious damage that the passage of several centuries can do is undoubtedly to blunt our response to the language which the characters use, and to the purposes for which they use it. Many people, it is true, don't care to admit that there is any real difficulty here, and are prepared to maintain that the only thing that matters is what Shakespeare's plays do for us, and not what they may have done for the Elizabethans. But the sad fact remains that when we read or hear a play of Shakespeare's we are, up to a point, consciously or unconsciously translating it, and what we get from it will depend, *inter alia*, on our ability to translate, in the widest possible sense of the word, from Elizabethan into modern English. The difficulties I have in mind are not so much those of vocabulary (words which may have become obsolete, or which have now required a different meaning), but those which affect the tone and attitude and intention of the various characters. Much of what they say is still perfectly clear to us, but on other occasions the effect aimed at by Shakespeare is obscured or even quite lost.

One of the chief reasons why the plays of Shakespeare sometimes fail to transmit their full meaning to us is the blank verse in which the greater part of each play is written. In his novel, *Sandra Belloni*, George Meredith allows one of his characters to make a sweeping generalization about French writers. 'Read their stereotyped descriptions,' this character says. 'They all say the same things. They have one big Gallic trumpet.'[1] This sort of observation might get by at a London cocktail party, but would seem very flippant and ill-informed in a Parisian café: it is the gay and irresponsible remark of someone who is not really familiar with French literature. In the same way, many people are inclined to think of the blank verse of Shakespeare and his contemporaries as one big Elizabethan trumpet. We might conceivably say something like that of Marlowe's *Tamburlaine*, but we could not possibly speak of Shakespeare's continuously varied and responsive blank verse in such terms. Yet, just as we are no longer familiar with the eighteenth-century heroic couplet and are apt to find it monotonous where the contemporaries of Pope and Dr. Johnson would have found subtle variation, so we are no longer really familiar with blank verse as a dramatic medium, and are apt to miss all sorts of nuances and distinctions of tone and emphasis. The way in which Shakespeare's blank verse is often spoken by the modern actor makes me feel sure that I am not inventing or exaggerating this particular difficulty.

To make things as hard for myself as possible, I hope to show some of those differences of tone and intention and emphasis by examing a play which is usually thought of as being the very essence of Elizabethan poetic drama: *Romeo and Juliet*. 'Read *Romeo and Juliet*,' Coleridge wrote, '—all is youth and spring; youth with all its follies, its virtues, its precipitancies; spring with its odours, its flowers, and its transiency; it is one and the same feeling that commences, goes through, and ends the play.' He goes on to note that in Juliet 'love has all that is tender and melancholy in the nightingale, all that is voluptuous in the rose, with whatever is sweet in the freshness of spring; but it ends with a long deep sigh like the last breeze of the Italian evening.'[2] This is, of course, a good example of that impressionistic criticism which is at present so much out of fashion:

[1] G. Meredith, *Sandra Belloni*, ch. viii.
[2] S. T. Coleridge, *Lectures and Notes on Shakespeare*, ed. T. Ashe, 1893, pp. 236–7.

one can well imagine the sort of punishment that would be meted out to any twentieth-century critic who wrote of *Romeo and Juliet* in such terms, always supposing that he could. Coleridge, at all events, concludes the passage with the statement that 'This unity of feeling and character pervades every drama of Shakespeare.' How true is that last sentence? And how true is it to say that 'it is one and the same feeling that commences, goes through, and ends' *Romeo and Juliet*? I am not so foolish as to wish to suggest that this tragedy does not leave a unified impression on the mind; but the Shakespearian unity is one that comprehends and reconciles much diversity.

The play does not open, as Coleridge's words might lead us to expect, with young Romeo and Juliet alone in an Italian garden while the moon shines through the fruit trees and a nightingale sings with her breast against a thorn. It opens with two very ordinary examples of the common man, Sampson and Gregory, servants in the house of Capulet. They spend some time in what we would now call passing remarks, they make some poor puns, and soon, with that inevitability which we come to associate with the common man in Shakespeare, they are making mildly bawdy jokes. The nearest that their talk gets to love is that it turns on sex. But this is not the sort of love that Coleridge meant; it certainly hasn't 'all that is tender and melancholy in the nightingale'. After a few minutes of this cross-talk, '*Enter* ABRAHAM *and* BALTHASAR', and almost at once the swords are out and the four men are fighting. All this, of course, is highly relevant to the tragedy that Shakespeare is writing; it brings us face to face with the bitter quarrel that divides the Montagues from the Capulets. But it is very different from the sort of opening we should get in a Greek tragedy or in a neo-classical one.

At this point various gentlemen come in: Benvolio, followed immediately by Tybalt, then Capulet in his gown, and finally Montague. Because they are gentlemen they all speak in blank verse, and not in the prose of their servants. It is the ordinary quarrelling speech of Shakespeare's upper-class characters; spirited, exclamatory, but none the less controlled and refined. While Lady Capulet and Lady Montague are striving to pacify them, the Prince enters with his attendants. He, too, speaks, of course, in blank verse. But does

Shakespeare differentiate his speech from that of his subjects? I think we must say that he does, and I believe that the Elizabethan playgoer would have recognized the distinction at once.

> *Prince.* Rebellious subjects, enemies to peace,
> Profaners of this neighbour-stainéd steel—
> Will they not hear?—What ho! you men, you beasts,
> That quench the fire of your pernicious rage
> With purple fountains issuing from your veins,
> On pain of torture, from those bloody hands
> Throw your mistemper'd weapons to the ground,
> And hear the sentence of your moved prince . . .
> (I. i. 87ff.)

It is, no doubt, only too easy to encourage ourselves to detect delicate gradations of style and tone where none exist, and to persuade ourselves, because we know that it is a prince who is talking to his subjects, that he is talking *like* a prince. But there is surely a special sort of grandiloquence in his manner of speaking; the voice of the ruler is clearly heard in such expressions as 'profaners of this neighbour-stainéd steel' (with its impressive compound-adjective), in 'the fire of your pernicious rage' quenched with 'purple fountains' of blood, and in his demand that they throw their 'mistemper'd weapons' to the ground. The diction is a little more artificial and polysyllabic than is normal. Shakespeare's kings and princes and dukes, too, are usually given a measured eloquence; they speak with a confident fullness of speech. I think we can detect this voice, the voice of authority, in Duke Theseus when he expresses his courteous willingness to listen to the rude play of the mechanicals (*Midsummer Night's Dream*, V. i), or in the various utterances of the banished duke in *As You Like It*. I admit that we are here in the region of imponderables, but rather than leave the point insufficiently demonstrated I will give one more example. Consider the speech of Duncan when he arrives with a large following of Scottish lords before Macbeth's castle, and the speech of Banquo that follows (I. vi. iff.):

> *Duncan.* This castle hath a pleasant seat; the air
> Nimbly and sweetly recommends itself
> Unto our gentle senses.
> *Banquo.* This guest of summer,
> The temple-haunting martlet, does approve,

> By his loved mansionry, that the heaven's breath
> Smells wooingly here: no jutty, frieze,
> Buttress, nor coign of vantage, but this bird
> Hath made his pendant bed and procreant cradle:
> Where they most breed and haunt, I have observed
> The air is delicate.

The first thing to be noticed here is the calm and controlled rhythm, the easy-flowing periods in which both the king and Banquo express their thoughts and feelings. No doubt there is often more than one good reason for anything in Shakespeare; and if I am told that this feeling of calm has tremendous dramatic significance in view of the horrid deed which is soon to take place within these walls, I shall be very ready to agree. But I would still contend that Duncan's gentle and equable speech is not only characteristic of this particular king who 'hath borne his faculties so meek', but is typical, in Shakespearian drama, of the man habituated to authority. More interesting, perhaps, in this context is the speech of Banquo; and here we have to consider not merely its rhythmical structure, but the very obvious heightening in the language. The house-martin is 'the guest of summer', it is 'temple-haunting' (again the compound adjective), its nest-building is its 'lov'd mansionry', and its nest is variously described as a 'pendant bed' and a 'procreant cradle'. Almost any eighteenth-century poet would have been delighted with himself if he had managed to coin such phrases, for if ever we had a case of poetic diction this is it. But why does Banquo, who usually talks in a much more natural fashion, suddenly take to this mode of speech? I think we must account for it by the fact that he is addressing his sovereign in the presence of the two royal princes and a number of the great Scottish noblemen. I may add that this heightened and artificial diction to which I have been calling attention was remarked upon by Alexander Pope. 'Shakespeare', he complained, 'generally used to stiffen his style with high words and metaphors for the speeches of his kings and great men: he mistook it for a mark of greatness.'[3] I don't think that Shakespeare's practice calls for complaint, and coming from the translator of Homer it may be thought that Pope's criticism is a case of the pot calling the kettle black; but

[3] Joseph Spence, *Anecdotes, Observations and Characters*, ed. S. W. Singer, 1820, p. 173.

at least Shakespeare's normal practice had not escaped Pope's observation.

When Shakespeare 'stiffened his style with high words and metaphors', he sometimes did so for quite a different reason: an artificial, elaborate and highly metaphorical style (the opposite of 'honest plain words') is sometimes, in the Shakespearian idiom, the sign of insincerity. An obvious example may be found in the hypocritical asseverations of Regan and Goneril, when the old king has asked his three daughters, 'Which of you shall we say doth love us most?' Regan, who is trying to outbid her sister, assures the king that Goneril

> names my very deed of love;
> Only she comes too short: that I profess
> Myself an enemy to all other joys,
> Which the most precious square of sense possesses;
> And find I am alone felicitate
> In your dear highness' love.
>
> (I. i. 39ff.)

The earliest use recorded in the O.E.D. for the word 'felicitate', which is the reverse of plain and in the context far from honest, is this passage in *King Lear*; it must have had a very artificial sound in Elizabethan ears. No commentator has ever given a satisfactory explanation of 'the most precious square of sense'; it looks like an emphatic and impressionistic improvisation of Regan's. Equally significant are the words that Shakespeare puts into the mouth of Iachimo when he first meets Imogen, and is already trying to poison her mind with half-expressed suggestions that her absent husband has been unfaithful to her. (*Cymb.*, I. vi. 39ff.):

> It cannot be i' the eye, for apes and monkeys
> 'Twixt two such shes would chatter this way and
> Contemn with mows the other; nor i' the judgement,
> For idiots in this case of favour would
> Be wisely definite; nor i' the appetite;
> Sluttery to such neat excellence opposed
> Should make desire vomit emptiness,
> Not so allured to feed.
>
> *Imo.* What is the matter, trow?
>
> *Iach.* The cloyed will,
> That satiate yet unsatisfied desire, that tub

Both fill'd and running, ravening first the lamb
Longs after for the garbage.

Imo. What, dear sir,
Thus raps you? Are you well?

Iachimo can speak simply enough on other occasions (although hardly any character except Imogen speaks simply for long at a time in this stylistically-fascinating play), and the words just quoted are loaded with insincerity, expressed not only by their intentional obscurity, but also by the tortured and crowded metaphors.

I come back now to *Romeo and Juliet.* Having rebuked his rebellious subjects, the Prince leaves the stage, and the talk turns on Romeo. Lady Montague asks if anyone has seen him, and Benvolio answers her (I. i. 124ff.):

Madam, an hour before the worshipp'd sun
Peer'd forth the golden window of the east,
A troubled mind drave me to walk abroad;
Where, underneath the grove of sycamore
That westward rooteth from the city's side,
So early walking did I see your son. . . .

We have already met Benvolio and heard him talk, and this is not his normal voice. It is true that he is addressing a noble lady, and might be expected on that account to put on what used to be called company manners. But that isn't it. Her husband, old Montague, takes up the tale in exactly the same high-flown and artificial strain:

Many a morning hath he there been seen,
With tears augmenting the fresh morning's dew,
Adding to clouds more clouds with his deep sighs;
But all so soon as the all-cheering sun
Should in the furthest east begin to draw
The shady curtains from Aurora's bed,
Away from light steals home my heavy son,
And private in his chamber pens himself. . . .

The speeches we have been noticing so far have all been 'in character', but these of Benvolio and Montague which I have just quoted must be accounted for on a different principle. While they do impart a certain amount of information about Romeo, they are primarily intended to make a direct emotional impression on the minds of the audience. The purpose of the highly-wrought language in these two speeches, with the sun peering forth from 'the golden window of the east' and drawing 'the shady curtains from Aurora's bed' is clearly to build up a romantic atmosphere for the first entrance of Romeo, who duly appears about a dozen lines later. The speeches of Benvolio and Montague, then, act in much the same way as dreamy incidental music to herald the entrance of the lover. What is actually said is not negligible, but it is the way of saying it that really matters here; the connotation of the words is more important than their denotation. Shakespeare often wrote such speeches, more particularly in his earliest plays, to provide an emotional setting, to act as a sort of verbal limelight for a character or an approaching event. Tamora's very Senecan speech in *Titus Andronicus* (II. iii. 93ff.), just before the murder of Bassianus and the ravishing and mutilation of Lavinia, is of this kind. 'A barren detested vale you see it is,' she tells Demetrius and Chiron, and she proceeds to darken the gloom by talking of the trees in full summer being 'forlorn and lean', the 'baleful mistleto', the 'nightly owl and fatal raven', 'a thousand hissing snakes, ten thousand swelling toads', the 'dismal yew' and so on. The Elizabethan playgoer knew that this could mean only one thing; he was prepared for the worst. On such occasions the most unlikely character may be called upon to provide the necessary creeps, and his words may be quite unnaturalistic and out of character. In *2 Henry VI* it is the captain of a pirate ship whose men are about to murder the Duke of Suffolk. The stage directions in the Folio read: '*Alarum. Fight at Sea. Ordnance goes off*', and then the captain enters and speaks (IV. i. 1ff.):

> The gaudy, blabbing and remorseful day
> Is crept into the bosom of the sea;
> And now loud-howling wolves arouse the jades
> That drag the tragic melancholy night;
> Who, with their drowsy, slow and flagging wings,
> Clip dead men's graves and from their misty jaws
> Breathe foul contagious darkness in the air.
> Therefore bring forth the soldiers of our prize;
> For, whilst our pinnace anchors in the Downs,
> Here shall they make their ransom on the sand,
> Or with their blood stain the discolour'd shore.

Put into naturalistic language, this would amount to saying: 'It is getting dark, so bring out the prisoners: they must either pay us ransom, or we shall kill them.' The significance of the captain's 'Therefore' is by no means clear: it looks like a *non sequitur*, unless he means that because it is now dark it is safe to bring out the prisoners. But we are wasting our time here if we look for a causal relation: Shakespeare is not thinking of cause but of effect—the effect that this loud, gloomy, vague and extravagant talk about loud-howling wolves and dead men's graves will have on the audience at the old Theatre in Shoreditch. The feeling which the captain's speech arouses is not really engendered by the situation, or by any conflict between character and circumstance, but is being deliberately pumped into the play at this point. It is not therefore a precise emotion, but it was never intended to be. What is needed here is a vague but powerful feeling of uneasiness and apprehension in the audience, and so the dramatist puts those wild and whirling words into the mouth of the poor captain, who is not so much a character as a dramatic convenience. It is true that *2 Henry VI* is very early work, and Shakespeare later learnt to manage such atmospheric effects much more subtly. Yet as late as *Macbeth* the bleeding sergeant who appears in Act I, scene ii, is another example of a character whose main function is to generate excitement while imparting some necessary information.

To return to *Romeo and Juliet*: Romeo now enters. Romeo is in love, not yet with Juliet, but with Rosaline, who is cold to him. He speaks in quite a different way from Benvolio, who is with him, and from Mercutio a little later. The talk of Shakespeare's young men who are in love almost invariably runs into every kind of excess and hyperbole. 'Now is he for the numbers that Petrarch flowed in,' says Mercutio as he sees the distracted Romeo coming towards him. In Shakespeare's world the young men normally pursue the young women, and endeavour to win them with a passionate eloquence. The young lover in Shakespeare therefore behaves like the blackbird or thrush; he sits on the topmost branch of the tree and sings to his mate. About the time that he wrote *Romeo and Juliet* Shakespeare gave us this human bird-song in the series of *arias* that he wrote for Valentine and Proteus in *The Two Gentlemen of Verona*, and again in

Love's Labour's Lost, where the king and his three gentlemen all break into extravagant protestations of their love for their respective ladies. Some years later Orlando in *As You Like It* is still the typical Shakespearian lover. Romeo is entirely in the tradition:

> Why, then, O brawling love! O loving hate!
> O any thing! of nothing first create!
> O heavy lightness! serious vanity!
> Mis-shapen chaos of well-seeming forms!
> Feather of lead, bright smoke, cold fire, sick health!
> Still-waking sleep, that is not what it is! . . .
>
> (I. i. 181ff.)

This is the Elizabethan lover, expressing himself in wild antitheses which are a sort of verbal equivalent for his distracted state balanced between two extremes ('feather of lead', 'cold fire', etc.), and in conceits ('Love is a smoke raised by the fume of sighs') which serve to represent the pleasing anguish of the lover, the grief of unrequited love which is yet a happier condition than not loving at all would be. Shakespeare may be writing in the Petrarchan convention on these occasions, but he uses it quite seriously in tragedy, and he makes good use of it in comedy when the intelligent young women who are the objects of this extravagant adoration calmly prick the iridescent bubbles which their lovers are blowing so beautifully.

This brings us to the end of the first scene, with Benvolio talking good sense and Romeo still raving. But already, in this one scene, we have had a considerable variety of speech because we have had a corresponding variety of life—low life and high life, rebellion and authority, romance and common sense.

The second scene, which opens with Capulet talking to Paris, offers us at first nothing that we have not had before. But then Capulet instructs one of his servants to deliver various invitations for the ball he is giving that evening, and the servant is a chuckle-headed fellow, who is, in fact, the equivalent of one of Shakespeare's blundering clowns, and who speaks like one. In his brief muddled soliloquy he is something quite different from the servants we met at the beginning of the play. Then we have Benvolio and Romeo again, much as before.

This brings us to scene iii, and to the Nurse. The Nurse in *Romeo and Juliet* is one of Shakespeare's earliest triumphs in character study. Granville-Barker, who was not given to extravagant statements, and who as a producer of plays was exceptionally alive to the sort of distinctions that we are here considering, said of this famous character: 'You may, indeed, take any sentence the Nurse speaks throughout the play, and only she could speak it.'[4] The Nurse expresses herself both in verse and in prose; but when it is in verse it is of so familiar and conversational a kind that it tends to disappear as verse almost as completely as the verse does in Swift's poem, 'The Humble Petition of Frances Harris'. When we first meet her with Lady Capulet there is some discussion about how old Juliet is. The Nurse is sure she is not fourteen yet, and asks how long it is till Lammas-tide (I. iii. 15ff.):

Lady Cap. A fortnight and odd days.
Nurse. Even or odd, of all days in the year,
Come Lammas-eve at night shall she be fourteen.
Susan and she—God rest all Christian souls!—
Were of an age: well, Susan is with God;
She was too good for me: but, as I said,
On Lammas-eve at night shall she be fourteen;
That shall she, marry; I remember it well.
'Tis since the earthquake now eleven years;
And she was wean'd—I never shall forget it—
Of all the days of the year, upon that day:
For I had then laid wormwood to my dug,
Sitting in the sun under the dove-house wall;
My lord and you were then at Mantua—
Nay, I do bear a brain—but, as I said,
When it did taste the wormwood on the nipple
Of my dug and felt it bitter, pretty fool,
To see it tetchy and fall out with the dug!
'Shake' quoth the dove-house: 'twas no need, I trow,
To bid me trudge:
And since that time it is eleven years;
For then she could stand alone; nay, by the rood,
She could have run and waddled all about;
For even the day before, she broke her brow:
And then my husband—God be with his soul!
'A was a merry man—took up the child:

Harley Granville-Barker, *Prefaces to Shakespeare: Second Series*, 1944, p. 42.

'Yea,' quoth he, 'dost thou fall upon thy face?
Thou wilt fall backward when thou hast more wit;
Wilt thou not, Jule?' and, by my holidame,
The pretty wench left crying and said 'Ay'.
To see, now, how a jest shall come about!
I warrant, an I should live a thousand years,
I never should forget it. 'Wilt thou not, Jule?' quoth he;
And, pretty fool, it stinted and said 'Ay.'

In trying to pin down what is characteristic in speech we have to take account of such considerations as the age, sex, social class and education of the speaker, and when we have allowed for all those there may not be much unaccounted for that we could attribute solely to the individual. The Nurse, for instance, has the garrulity of old age, and a tendency to slide into reminiscence. She recalls the earthquake, and that she was sitting in the sun under the dove-house wall when it happened, and that her master and mistress were away in Mantua at the time, and what her husband said when Juliet fell, and much else of the same purely factual kind. She has the animal vitality of healthy old age: once she is off on a reminiscence she is as irrepressible as the Wife of Bath, and has the same hearty vulgarity and confident feminity. Her lack of education is seen in the way that she joins her narrative together with a series of 'Ands' and 'Buts' and 'Fors', the 'Buts' and 'Fors' being usually no more than simple connectives, and not really adversative or causal. She is endlessly repetitive, sometimes consciously so ('But, as I said'), more often unconsciously. (Her husband's brilliant joke, 'Wilt thou not, Jule?' is repeated for the third time in her next speech.) She has the uneducated speaker's constant striving for emphasis, obtained characteristically by means of oaths ('marry', 'by the rood'), by her wager, 'I'll lay fourteen of my teeth', and by frequent exclamations ('God rest all Christian souls!', 'pretty fool!', 'God be with his soul!'). She keeps interrupting herself, breaking off as some irrelevant idea enters her head, i.e. some idea accidentally associated in time or place with what she is saying ('Well, Susan is with God', 'For even a day before, she broke her brow'). Her whole speech, of course, is one vast irrelevance: the sole point at issue is the question: How old is Juliet? On this point, since I have quoted Coleridge at his most impressionistic, let me now quote him at his most psychological. 'In all her recollections,' Coleridge said of the Nurse, 'she assists herself by the remembrance of visual circumstances. The great difference, in this respect, between the cultivated and the uncultivated mind is this—that the cultivated mind will be found to recall the past by certain regular trains of cause and effect; whereas, with the uncultivated mind, the past is recalled wholly by coincident images, or facts which happened at the same time.'[5] Linguistically, the words and phrases the Nurse uses have often the marks of popular speech. I am not sure about 'dug'. Although, as the O.E.D. tells us, the word 'as applied to a woman's breast [is] now contemptuous', it could have been used quite inoffensively in the 1590s by Queen Elizabeth or the Dark Lady of the Sonnets. But there is no question of the colloquial nature of 'That shall she, marry', ''A was a merry man', or ''twas no need, I trow, to bid me trudge'. To get the modern equivalent of this last remark we should have to substitute something like 'You bet there was no need to tell *me* to hop it.'

The Nurse, then, is a highly recognizable character. As such, she brings us to the teasing question of how far Shakespeare was able to individualize his characters by giving them a unique, or at least personal, mode of expression. Can we recognize, say, Falstaff, Cleopatra, Antony, Richard II, Richard III, Shylock, Caliban, Hamlet, Hotspur, Shallow, Coriolanus, Malvolio, Iago by the way they talk? Large claims of this kind have been made by critics of many periods. Pope asserted that 'every single character in Shakespeare is as much an Individual as those in Life itself; it is impossible to find any two alike'. And he went on to say: 'Had all the Speeches been printed without the very names of the Persons, I believe one might have apply'd them with certainty to every speaker.'[6] This is surely the language of exaggeration. However well my students may know *Macbeth*, I hate to think what they would do to me if I set them an essay in which I asked them to contrast the characters of Lenox and Ross as they are revealed by their speeches. Yet most of us probably feel that what Pope says of all Shakespeare's characters is at least true of many of them.

[5] *Lectures and Notes on Shakespeare, ed. cit.*, p. 87.

[6] *Eighteenth Century Essays on Shakespeare*, ed. D. Nichol Smith, 2nd ed., 1963, p. 45.

> Come on, come on, come on, sir; give me your hand, sir, give me your hand, sir: an early stirrer, by the rood! . . . Jesu, Jesu, the mad days that I have spent! and to see how many of my old acquaintance are dead! . . . Certain, 'tis certain; very sure, very sure: death, as the Psalmist saith, is certain to all; all shall die. How a good yoke of bullocks at Stamford fair?

In those words[7] we recognize at once the quavering effervescence of Mr. Justice Shallow, still on this side of senility, but already a *laudator temporis acti*, and much given to repetition, but a kind of repetition which is quite different from that of the Nurse, and is indeed a characteristic expression of his mellow exuberance. I have always supposed that Shakespeare wrote the part of Shallow for an actor with a reedy piping voice, and my reasons for thinking so are not only the words he puts into Shallow's mouth, but the obvious contrast that is intended between Shallow and Silence. On the few occasions when Silence gets in a word at all, it is to say things like 'Alas, a black ouzel, cousin Shallow', or 'Dead, sir', or 'We shall all follow, cousin', and those gloomy and taciturn remarks seem to demand a deep bass. When, immediately afterwards, Shallow and Falstaff are together on the stage, the deep voice of Falstaff rumbling up from his stomach seems again to require a contrasting tenor from the eager, scatter-brained Shallow.

To turn for a moment to a quite different character, it is interesting to find Dryden saying of Caliban that Shakespeare has 'most judiciously furnished him with a person, a language, and a character which will suit him, both by father's and mother's side . . . His language is as hobgoblin as his person.'[8] The difficulty begins when we try to go beyond such general statements to an analysis of Caliban's mode of speech. When Browning wrote 'Caliban upon Setebos' he gave Caliban a highly individual utterance by exaggerating certain syntactical peculiarities designed to leave an impression of uncouthness. Shakespeare's Caliban is far less heavily underlined, but we still feel that he has a peculiar way of speaking. A. W. Schlegel gives us a clue when he points out that Caliban 'has picked up everything dissonant and thorny in language, to compose out of

[7] *2 Henry IV*, III. ii. 1ff.

[8] *Essays of John Dryden*, ed. W. P. Ker, 1900, vol. i, pp. 219, 220.

it a vocabulary of his own'.[9] Caliban's first speech is, in fact, a prolonged curse, as is his next one, with its imprecation, 'Toads, beetles, bats light on you.' Still cursing in Act II, scene ii, he speaks of infections from bogs and fens, pinches, urchins, apes mowing and chattering and biting him, hedgehogs pricking his bare feet. There is much imagery natural to a savage; he refers to the sun and moon as 'the bigger light and the less'. But he has, too, one lovely speech (III. ii. 147ff.):

> Be not afeard: the isle is full of noises,
> Sounds and sweet airs, that give delight and hurt not . . .

All this builds up into a complex impression, from which we can easily persuade ourselves that we can recognize the voice of Caliban.

Shylock, again, is recognizably a Jew, although he is more lightly scored than the modern stage Jew would probably be. Still, he uses words and phrases that, whether specifically Jewish or not, differentiate him from the Christians. But this is not just any Jew, it is Shylock; and to account for what it is in his speech that makes him uniquely Shylock is the ultimate challenge to the linguistic critic. The traditional tools of criticism can help us to some sort of answer, but ultimately I think we shall have to look elsewhere for a solution. I belong myself to the pre-computer age, and look with a sort of nervous admiration at those of my younger colleagues for whom such things are part of the ordinary stock in trade of the scholar; but the computer probably holds a good part of the answer to our questions. If, in addition to coping with the words and phrases that Shakespeare's characters use, it can also be coaxed into distinguishing between the dominant rhythms in the speech of an Antony, a Richard III, a Hotspur and a Lear, we shall be very near the heart of the mystery.

I return to *Romeo and Juliet*. In Act I, scene iv, we meet Mercutio, a young gentleman of fashion, gay, mocking, *not* in love. His conversation, with a good deal of *double entendre* and some polished phrases, anticipates in places the talk of the libertine gallant of Restoration comedy. For Shakespeare he is almost unique, but

[9] A. W. Schlegel, *Lectures on Dramatic Art and Literature*, trans. John Black, 1846, p. 395.

Mercutio would have found many young men like himself in the plays of Fletcher. The character in Shakespeare who most resembles him is perhaps the irrepressible Lucio in *Measure for Measure*, a young man quite distinct from Mercutio, and yet in his free-spoken and irresponsible way talking very much 'according to the trick'.

In scene v we have Capulet again, the very picture of fussy and bustling old age, welcoming his guests with an old-world courtesy and recalling the feats of his dancing youth. But Tybalt has caught sight of Romeo, and complains to his uncle. The old man doesn't want trouble at his party, and tries to pacify him. 'I'll not endure him,' Tybalt says. Capulet now loses his temper (I. v. 80ff.):

Cap. He shall be endured:
What, goodman boy! I say, he shall: go to;
Am I the master here, or you? go to.
You'll not endure him! God shall mend my soul!
You'll make a mutiny among my guests!
You will set cock-ahoop! You'll be the man!
Tyb. Why, uncle, 'tis a shame.
Cap. Go to, go to;
You are a saucy boy: is't so, indeed?
This trick may chance to scathe you, I know what:
You must contrary me! marry, 'tis time.—
Well said, my hearts!—You are a princox; go:
Be quiet, or—More light, more light!—For shame!
I'll make you quiet.—What, cheerly, my hearts!

When I spoke earlier of Shakespeare's continuously varied and responsive blank verse it was this sort of passage that I had in mind. The secret of it lies in a sort of contrapuntal effect between the formal rhythm of the pentameter line and the rhythm of colloquial speech. ('He *shall be* endured' . . . '*You'll* not endure him' . . . '*You'll* be the *man*!') In Capulet's second speech the effect is further heightened by his carrying on three conversations at once, with the mutinous Tybalt, with his guests as they pass by, and with his servants. Shakespeare's ability to accommodate his verse to every movement of passion grows more and more wonderful as his art matures. One thinks of the famous quarrel between Brutus and Cassius in *Julius Caesar* (IV. iii. 1ff.), Othello's furious retort to Lodovico, who has asked him to call Desdemona back (IV. i. 264ff.):

Sir, she can turn, and turn, and yet go on,
And turn again; and she can weep, sir, weep;
And she's obedient, as you say, obedient,
Very obedient. . . .

or the passionate outburst of the jealous Leontes in *The Winter's Tale*: 'Is whispering nothing? . . .' (I. ii. 284ff.), or the angry reiteration of Paulina in the same play (II. iii. 59ff.): 'Good queen, my lords, good queen; I say, good queen. . . .'

The last passage in *Romeo and Juliet* to which I wish to draw attention occurs in the famous second scene of Act II, when Romeo is in Capulet's orchard, and Juliet at her window. It needs little comment, but it illustrates another permanent principle in Shakespeare's dialogue. Romeo's language is still that of the passionate lover (II. ii. 26ff.):

O, speak again, bright angel! for thou art
As glorious to this night, being o'er my head,
As is a winged messenger of heaven
Unto the white-upturned wond'ring eyes
Of mortals that fall back to gaze on him
When he bestrides the lazy-pacing clouds,
And sails upon the bosom of the air. . . .

In complete contrast to this, the words of Juliet have the natural sincerity that almost invariably characterizes the speech of Shakespeare's young women in love (II. ii. 62ff.):

How camest thou hither, tell me, and wherefore?
The orchard walls are high and hard to climb,
And the place death, considering who thou art,
If any of my kinsmen find thee here.

Rom. With love's light wings did I o'er-perch these walls;
For stony limits cannot hold love out,
And what love can do that dares love attempt,
Therefore thy kinsmen are no let to me.

Jul. If they do see thee, they will murder thee.

Rom. Alack! there lies more peril in thine eye
Than twenty of their swords: look thou but sweet,
And I am proof against their enmity.

Jul. I would not for the world they saw thee here.

Shakespeare's young women, in contrast to his young men, are astonishingly sensible and practical; and when they are in love, as almost all of them are, they speak what we have no difficulty in recognizing as the language of the heart. But, however different the mode, Romeo's is also the language of the heart, or, more precisely, an Elizabethan literary equivalent for that language; and since life often learns from literature, no doubt some Elizabethan lovers wooed their mistresses in a style that approximated to that of Romeo.

With all this variety of speech from one character to another, and even in one character when the circumstances are different, there are certain ways of individualizing the speech of his men and women that Shakespeare avails himself of only lightly. Dialect, which is common enough in the work of some of his contemporaries and in Restoration and eighteenth-century drama, appears very seldom in Shakespeare's plays. The mechanicals in *A Midsummer Night's Dream* use the phrases of humble life, e.g. 'a proper man as one shall see in a summer's day', 'every mother's son', 'Masters', and so on, but you could not tell from the words they use what part of the country they live in. No doubt the actor who played Bottom gave him some sort of regional identity, but all that Shakespeare has indicated is that he comes from the artisan class. When he does attempt dialect in *Henry V* the results are not entirely happy. Fluellen and Sir Hugh Evans may pass for Welshmen, but Captain Jamy is only the merest shadow of a Scotsman. It is true that Katharine speaks quite good stage French, and the French Doctor in *The Merry Wives* speaks what has always been recognized on the English stage as the English that a Frenchman would speak. But those are, in Shakespeare, exceptions.

Nor does he show much interest in bringing out a man's profession by his mode of speech. Later seventeenth- and eighteenth-century comedy is full of the professional jargon of parsons, lawyers, sailors, shopkeepers and so on, but Shakespeare has little of it. It is true that the Boatswain in *The Tempest* gives his orders like a genuine sailor. Ancient Pistol (once more in *Henry V*) gives us a special sort of soldier talk, and Holofernes in *Love's Labour's Lost* is a pedant schoolmaster; but Sir Nathaniel in the same comedy is not a typical curate, and although Dogberry's speech is certainly individualized, it is hardly the talk of a typical constable.

How Roman are Shakespeare's Romans? There is a Ciceronian eloquence in the Antony of *Julius Caesar*, and an air of solid gravity in Brutus; but perhaps Ben Jonson came nearer to the true Roman fashion in his *Sejanus*. Still less does Shakespeare differentiate his Greeks from his Trojans in *Troilus and Cressida*. But how should he? How could he possibly know? If we ask for such distinctions we are asking him to guess. I think we must accept Dr. Johnson's reply to Dennis and Rymer, who had argued that Shakespeare's Romans were not sufficiently Roman. 'Shakespeare', says Johnson, 'always makes nature predominate over accident; and if he preserves the essential character is not very careful of distinctions superinduced and adventitious. His story requires Romans . . ., but he thinks only on men.'[10]

Let us take a last look at Shakespeare doing just that. It is the scene on Pompey's galley in *Antony and Cleopatra*. Antony is talking to Caesar about the Nile and the pyramids of Egypt, and Lepidus, who has been drinking heavily, listens in a state of befuddlement. He now pulls himself together, and speaks (II. vii. 29ff.):

Lep. Your serpent of Egypt is bred now of your mud by the operation of your sun: so is your crocodile.
Ant. They are so.
Pomp. Sit,—and some wine! A health to Lepidus!
Lep. I am not so well as I should be, but I'll ne'er out. . . . Nay, certainly, I have heard that Ptolemies' pyramises are very goodly things; without contradiction I have heard that. . . . What manner o' thing is your crocodile?
Ant. It is shaped, sir, like itself; and it is as broad as it hath breadth: it is just so high as it is, and moves with its own organs . . .
Lep. What colour is it of?
Ant. Of its own colour too.
Lep. 'Tis a strange serpent.

Here we have Shakespeare tampering magnificently with history, and caring little whether Lepidus and Antony are Romans, so long as they are men. Lepidus, his legs and his wits slithering away together from under him until he is finally carried drunk ashore, is a beautiful study in progressive intoxication. As always in Shakespeare, the words are right; and the words are right because by

[10] *Eighteenth Century Essays on Shakespeare, ed. cit.*, p. 109.

some sort of empathy in the dramatist the thing that they express has been completely experienced. 'The great secret of morals', wrote Shelley, 'is love'; and for Shelley love meant a going out of our own nature and an identification of ourselves with the thoughts and actions and persons of other people. 'A man, to be greatly good,' he believed, 'must imagine intensely and comprehensively; he must put himself in the place of another and of many others; the pains and pleasures of his species must become his own.'[11] In his own intense way Shelley realized some part of his own ideal; but if we are to name the supreme example of an imaginative writer to whom the pains and pleasures of his species became his own, that writer is Shakespeare.

I have been discussing words, language, modes of speech, and it may be thought that I have chosen a topic that is not sufficiently central to Shakespeare's great achievement. Yet it is only through those words, that language, and those modes of speech that Shakespeare was able to people the English stage with the most remarkable company of characters in all dramatic literature; and the words never failed him—whether they were for a Lear in the storm or a Juliet at the casement, a Cleopatra putting the asp to her bosom, or poor silly Lepidus babbling about crocodiles aboard Pompey's galley.

[11] *English Critical Essays: Nineteenth Century* ('A Defence of Poetry'), ed. Edmund D. Jones, 1916, p. 132.

VII

Shakespeare's Language

HILDA HULME

IN *The Comedy of Errors*, Shakespeare's play about the two pairs of identical twins, Dromio of Syracuse, who is mistaken for his brother, tells of how he is claimed in marriage by Nell, the kitchen-wench. He says: 'I am due to a woman: One that claimes me, one that haunts me, one that will haue me.' It is a pleasant fancy that, in this pitiful complaint of Dromio, Shakespeare himself is speaking in allegory to those who will come after him. He seems to be expressing his own fear at the possibility that linguist and textual critic of future centuries may so confidently hang about him, so claim and haunt him. Perhaps, too, as literary artist, he is speculating rather unkindly on the best use that might be made of later critical interpretation. Dromio describes the presumptuous Nell in these words:

> Marry sir, she's the Kitchin wench, & al grease, and I know not what vse to put her too, but to make a Lampe of her, and run from her by her owne light. I warrant, her ragges and the Tallow in them, will burne a Poland Winter: if she liues till doomesday, she'l burne a weeke longer then the whole World (III. ii. 96ff.).

It is unnecessary to linger over the darker meanings of this passage. Few of us at the present time can rest undaunted as we contemplate the sheer bulk of textual and linguistic commentary that has accumulated about Shakespeare's writings, and yet we are all quite well aware that there has never been any danger of Shakespeare himself being 'buried under the load of his commentators'.[1] We recognize on the one hand, that no composite effort of more than two centuries of scholarship can buy us admission to the theatre of Shakespeare's

[1] *The Plays and Poems of William Shakespeare*, ed. Edmund Malone, 1790, vol. I, p. lvii.

day; we can never hope to bring to his language a complete and instinctive understanding, the imaginative yet accurate apprehension of an Elizabethan audience; many factors of linguistic change in the ten or so generations which separate us from the speech-community of Shakespeare's world must cloud our appreciation of the finer detail of the language which he 'made'. But there is a sense also in which the Elizabethan dramatist, through the words of his characters, can speak directly to men of every nation and of every age; his art and language have a certain universal appeal; the essence of his meaning is still communicated; the energy of his expression has an ever-living power. And it seems fitting, therefore, in speaking of Shakespeare's achievement four centuries after his birth, to consider first not what is Elizabethan in his language, but what constitutes its common appeal.

Many readers have surely felt that art of the quality which Shakespeare offers needs no interpreter; the subject of such art is our common human experience—the never-changing reality of man's awareness of his nature, an awareness which can include the crudest formulations of malice and self-seeking as well as a truer and nobler consciousness of what we are to ourselves and to each other. The unique power of the artist is to show, within the little moment of the individual life, the whole history of that knowledge which man has won from darkness, and which is won afresh in every mind and heart. About Picasso, who is perhaps the Shakespeare of our present century, the story is told of how one day he was walking in Paris and saw a learned man sitting on a bench in a public garden. And he said to his companion, 'Look at that face, it is as old as the world, all faces are as old as the world.'[2] Shakespeare's language is, in this sense, as old as the world. His power to embody in dramatic form the eternal truths of our human existence was recognized in his own day by his fellow actors; they speak of him as 'a happie imitator of Nature'.[3] Ben Jonson, who, of Shakespeare's contemporaries, was most qualified to appreciate his comprehensive realism, gives him the most generous praise when he says, 'Nature her selfe was proud

[2] Gertrude Stein, *Picasso*, 1938, p. 13.

[3] John Heminge and Henrie Condell, Prefatory address 'To the great Variety of Readers', First Folio, 1623.

of his designes.'[4] What was timeless in Shakespeare's art spoke then as now, and the manner in which he sets forth his 'excellent Phantsie' and 'brave notions'[5] compels at all times a living responsiveness from his readers and audience. We are conscious perhaps that much of his wisdom was never new, but his expression of that wisdom seems as though it will never grow old. To give an example of this: we never tire of quoting from his plays what we have turned into the most commonplace of sayings, torn from their context and many times repeated. Those who are ambitious remind themselves:

> There is a Tide in the affayres of men,
> Which taken at the Flood, leades on to Fortune.[6]

And we feel still the mystery of death in that

> vndiscouered Countrey, from whose Borne
> No Traueller returnes.[7]

When we read Shakespeare's plays in schools and colleges, we are brought up at once against the language barrier. Students are asked such questions as this: Give the meaning of the following in good modern English, paying special attention to the italicized words and phrases, and explaining the metaphor in lines 4 and 5. Exercises of this kind have their value, but only as a preparation for that deeper understanding of Shakespeare's language continuously acquired from youth to age, as we build into our lives the experience derived from art and see that art afresh as life brings new experiences. As T. S. Eliot said on his seventieth birthday, 'It takes a lifetime to grow up to Shakespeare.' Individual suffering or personal circumstance may give us new insight into Shakespeare's meaning. After the death of one's own father, *Hamlet* is a different play. Regan's words in *King Lear* (II. iv. 204), 'I pray you Father being weake, seeme so', have only cruelty, but we find, as it were, a footnote to her text, making the cruelty perhaps less personal, in many real-life situations. There are occasions when, for example, we stand powerless in all our strength before the iron resolution of some fragile and brittle old

[4] Ben Jonson, Prefatory verses, First Folio, 1623.
[5] Ben Jonson, *Timber: or Discoveries*, 1641, p. 98.
[6] *Julius Caesar*, IV. iii. 218f.
[7] *Hamlet*, III. ii. 79f.

lady—for my part I find old ladies more stubborn than old men—and in such moments we appreciate more keenly the extreme economy of Shakespeare's writing. No amount of exasperation could justify our speaking Regan's words, but it comforts us a little to hold their controlled compression in the hinterland of thought. And this way of writing, it seems to me, is not primarily Elizabethan; the precise handling of language is simply that of the master-artist of any age.

In the passage from Ben Jonson which I cited earlier, he praises Shakespeare's language both for its richness of texture and for its exact appropriateness. Nature, he says,

> ioy'd to weare the dressing of his lines!
> Which were so richly spun, and wouen so fit,
> As, since, she will vouchsafe no other Wit.[8]

We may accept, I think, that lines which are 'richly spun' have their most vivid life and colour in the time and place of their spinning: it is through a knowledge of Elizabethan idiom that we shall best appreciate the richness of detail in Shakespeare's poetry and prose. But the aptness of his expression, his power to create a language fitly woven, wholly suited to the intentions, explicit and implicit, both of speaker and of playwright, can make its full effect through words of sparse simplicity. Many passages could be quoted to illustrate this. I shall take here one passage—nine lines long in the Folio text—from the beginning of the sleep-walking scene of *Macbeth* (V. i. 16ff.), where the gentlewoman is questioned by the doctor, and I shall examine the dialogue in some detail, so as to show how, through what seems quite ordinary and artless language, Shakespeare brings before us the very form and likeness of the speaking-character. The scene begins:

> *Enter a Doctor of Physicke, and a Wayting Gentlewoman.*
>
> *Doct.* I haue too Nights watch'd with you, but can perceiue no truth in your report. When was it shee last walk'd?
>
> *Gent.* Since his Maiesty went into the Field, I haue

[8] Prefatory verses, First Folio, 1623.

seene her rise from her bed, throw her Night-Gown vp-
pon her, vnlocke her Closset, take foorth paper, folde it,
write vpon't, read it, afterwards Seale it, and againe re-
turne to bed; yet all this while in a most fast sleepe.

Doct. A great perturbation in Nature, to receyue at
once the benefit of sleep, and do the effects of watching.
In this slumbry agitation, besides her walking, and other
actuall performances, what (at any time) haue you heard
her say?

Gent. That Sir, which I will not report after her.

Doct. You may to me, and 'tis most meet you should.

Gent. Neither to you, nor any one, hauing no witnesse
to confirme my speech. *Enter Lady, with a Taper.*
Lo you, heere she comes: This is her very guise, and vpon my life fast asleepe: obserue her, stand close.

Doct. How came she by that light?

Gent. Why it stood by her: she ha's light by her continually, 'tis her command.

It seems at first sight that the Gentlewoman is there only to give information: she must let us know that since Macbeth 'went into the Field' his wife has begun sleep-walking, and so as to avoid spoiling the suspense of the latter part of the scene she must refuse to tell us the kind of thing that is said by the sleep-walker. But the manner of her refusal is wholly true to type and tone. The doctor has reflected, as doctors will, on the interest of the case, 'A great perturbation in Nature . . .', but has ended, again as doctors will, with a precise and unwelcome question: '. . . what (at any time) haue you heard her say?' Even to attempt analysis of the way in which their dialogue continues is 'to labour on a cobweb': we all know how necessary it is for the subordinate, and especially the female subordinate, to keep her dignity by keeping her place, transcending the limits of her subordination by a serene and absolute refusal to step beyond those limits. The gentlewoman, then, concedes the doctor's authority; she addresses him as *Sir* and she repeats the word *report* which he had used earlier: 'I haue too Nights watch'd with you, but can perceiue no truth in your report.' But what was a medical noun, has become, in her reply, a negative verb, on both professional and human grounds. Where the doctor had the dispassionate 'can perceiue no truth' she has made a choice, 'will not report after her';

'after her' implies the possibility of something discreditable in her mistress, but to 'report after her' would be dishonourable in her lady attendant. The doctor makes no comment on her scruples and offers no reaction to the repeated word 'report'; the arrogance in his 'You may to me' is male, legitimate, professional, but he is losing height a little in the second half of the line. It cannot be quite consonant with what he sees as the dignity of his position that he should need the superlative of ''tis most meet you should'. The gentlewoman, wholly without offensiveness, counters this superlative with one of her own and, so to say, acknowledging her awareness of his claim to be a special case, includes him none the less in her general negation, 'Neither to you, nor any one . . .' And she offers a new reason for her silence, 'hauing no witnesse to confirme my speech', which the doctor who 'can perceiue no truth' in her earlier report will not be able to set aside. This second reason is not the same as the first; that is to say, she argues like a woman (if I may express this in a phonetic metaphor, she uses diphthongs rather than vowels); she does not keep her points clearly separated, but reinforces the first argument of professional and personal loyalty, which is part reason and part emotion, with a second argument brought out perhaps with some feeling of triumph, as if she senses that its higher thought content must carry more weight against a male opponent. With the entrance of the sleep-walker her tone changes; divergent interests of doctor and attendant re-converge; the doctor is 'you', not 'Sir', and she gives *him* directions. To put it crudely, she is now in charge of the show and half enjoying the drama: 'This is her very guise, and vpon my life fast asleepe.' In the doctor's pertinent and unelaborated question 'How came she by that light?' the possibility of the patient's self-injury is foreshadowed, and the gentlewoman's reply, 'Why it stood by her', is the reaction of a woman whose world, for the moment, is entirely taken up by the present crisis and who is infinitely surprised that there should be other worlds which know nothing of the details of her problem. In this passage, it seems to me, the expression is totally appropriate; nothing could appear more natural; energy of speaking characters, and of creating dramatist, is firmly and quietly controlled. Doctor and gentlewoman have each their several identity; in their brevity of speech they show a fine awareness of who and what they are. It is clear also how appropriately this kind of language, the more forceful because more narrowly channelled, prepares us for the appearance of the sleep-walker. She who is now without identity (we may note the stage-direction: *Enter Lady, with a Taper*)—who is no longer Lady Macbeth and who is spoken of as the Queen only after her death—can find no way but one to

> Cleanse the stufft bosome, of that perillous stuffe
> Which weighes vpon the heart.
>
> (V. iii. 44.)

I have dealt so far with the universal appeal of Shakespeare's language. But great works of art, as well as having universal meaning, have also their special significance for different centuries. The habits of thought of a particular period condition the way in which these works are approached, and are reflected in the interpretations which are given to them. It is, we may agree, the special condition of our present age to be more than usually interested in what Shakespeare is able to accomplish through the language of imagery. The twentieth-century world is explicitly aware of the value of apprehending experience through fantasy: contemporary art in certain fields makes no clear distinction between image and reality. Films, plays and paintings sometimes show us image and symbol brought out from the world of feeling to be set down plainly before us as solid objects of the material world. A trick of the camera or of studio lighting and the winter in the heart of a forsaken wife shows itself as snow on the summer trees. In a most successful recent play, which deals with the involvements of domestic life, an actress speaks her part buried in sand, to above the waist in Act I, and up to her neck in Act II.[9] And for many years now Picasso and others have made it natural for us to see a human head at once full-face and in profile. As we become accustomed to new modes of expression in the art of today, we see, or think we see, new elements of structure and design in the art of the past. To take an example from modern painting: we find in some of the pictures of Braque a clear division of component objects into two halves, dark and light. By this means the artist is able to suggest the roundness of the object without the

[9] Samuel Beckett, *Happy Days*, 1962.

usual device of shading or tonal painting. Such paintings may prepare us to see in new terms what Shakespeare is doing in his structuring of *King Lear*. To explain this briefly: the real-life relationship of father and child is always changing. The child must grow, over the years, into an independent creature, needing no longer, as the young child does, to see all the light of the world in the love which its parents give. But the parent, meanwhile, losing independence as old age comes, can scarcely avoid making too large a claim on the child's affections. The father cannot wholly free his daughter; the old man, facing death, may become again the selfish child; remembering what he gave, he may claim too high a return, so that the earlier relationship is no longer clear and simple but shaded with pain and sorrow; love is darkened with hate. Many writers have dealt with the complexities of this theme in a realistic manner (notably Turgenev in his *Fathers and Sons*), but Shakespeare in *King Lear* chooses, like Braque, not shading, but contrast. He makes a clear-cut division between love and hate, light and darkness. Cordelia is almost wholly good; Goneril and Regan are shown as wholly evil. As we see or read the play we *feel* that we understand some of the reasons why Shakespeare has chosen this particular design, but it is hard to capture or express that feeling in the ordinary language of intellectual argument. These paintings of Braque express it for us. By this division into light and dark he is able, without shading, to suggest the roundness of the object. So, it seems to me, Shakespeare is able, through the formalized characters of his drama, wholly good and wholly evil, to suggest the many complexities of real-life relationship.

In yet another way Picasso's cubist portraits are a vivid reminder that any single interpretation of a work of art is likely to be insufficient for the modern mind. We can look in several ways at once at the one object. New truths blend in with the old. The way in which we regard the ending of *King Lear* is a case in point. Many readers see in the death of Cordelia 'the final grotesque horror in the play'. In the words of Wilson Knight, the 'tragedy is most poignant in that it is purposeless, unreasonable'.[10] In a not very well-known passage, Freud has given a new interpretation to the tragedy. He sees the story as an ancient myth, in which Cordelia has two roles, as the

[10] G. Wilson Knight, *The Wheel of Fire*, 1949, p. 174.

Goddess of Death, and as the Goddess of Love. In the earliest form of the myth the three sisters represent the three Fates, with Cordelia originally the Goddess of Death. But as man's mind rebelled against the discovery that he, too, is a part of nature and subject therefore to the immutable law that all things die, the myth was changed. The Goddess of Death was replaced by the Goddess of Love and by what was equivalent to her in human shape, the fairest, best and most lovable of women. And in the moving final scene, when Lear carries Cordelia's body on to the stage, Cordelia is death once more. To quote Freud,

> She is the Death-goddess who, like the Valkyrie in German mythology, carries away the dead hero from the battlefield. Eternal wisdom, clothed in the primaeval myth, bids the old man renounce love, choose death, and make friends with the necessity of dying.[11]

It will be clear, of course, that there is no final sense in which such interpretation is true or untrue, but it may well bring to some present-day readers a new imaginative insight into the potential meaning of the Elizabethan play.

I come now to what is specifically Elizabethan in Shakespeare's language. First, there is no doubt that the rich variety of life and speech in Elizabethan London provided Shakespeare and his fellow dramatists with the best of material and the finest of opportunities. People of all regions and all social classes were flocking to the city, gentlemen from all the shires, the younger sort, as Stow tells us, 'to see and shew vanity, and the elder to save the cost and charge of Hospitality, and house keeping'. Tradesmen and handicraftsmen followed, leaving the country towns, knowing that they would 'be sure to finde ready and quicke market' in the neighbourhood of the court, which was now 'much greater & more gallant then in former times'.[12] There are references to foolish country folk who wanted to change themselves into people of fashion, and in the extensive rogue literature of the time we read of many a country bumpkin falling a victim to the coneycatchers, the tricksters of the metropolis. Such a one had only to open his mouth, it seems, and guessing by his

[11] 'The Theme of the Three Caskets', Standard edition of *Works*, vol. xii, p. 301.
[12] John Stow, *A Survay of London*, 1603, p. 563.

tongue what country man he was, one of the gang would immediately claim acquaintance with him.

All classes of people, and not merely the confidence tricksters, were more than usually aware of the language differences within their common speech. London was the cultural centre, 'the fountaine whose riuers flowe round about England', the natural home of the developing standard language. And this standard language was a matter of *national* prestige: Nashe, in 1592, praises the poets of the time that 'they haue cleansed our language from barbarisme' and so made the ordinary people of London 'aspire to a richer puritie of speach' than could be found in any other nation.[13] Puttenham, in 1589, in his *Arte of English Poesie*, a critical analysis of the poet's craft, gives clear expression to the generally accepted linguistic theory: the language of the poet or maker is to be

> naturall, pure, and the most vsuall of all his countrey: and for the same purpose rather that which is spoken in the kings Court, or in the good townes and Cities within the land. . . .[14]

The poet is not to write in the terms of northern men, 'such as they vse in dayly talke', since their language is 'not so Courtly nor so currant as our Southerne English is', nor is he to use the speech of the far western man. His language is to be based on 'the vsuall speach of the Court, and that of London and the shires lying about London within lx myles, and not much aboue'. When we use the term 'Standard English' at the present time we are sometimes thinking only of a style of pronunciation, once the exclusive possession of a favoured social group, a matter of the right accent for the right job. But in Shakespeare's world, the developing standard language allowed a much greater variety of pronunciation than is heard today in the different types of educated speech. We are told of Sir Walter Ralegh that 'notwithstanding his so great mastership in style and his conversation with the learnedst and politest persons, yet he spake broad Devonshire to his dyeing day'.[15] What was important was the 'apt declaring of a mans mind'; he must use 'such wordes as are

[13] *Pierce Penilesse, His Supplication to the Diuell,* D3v.

[14] George Puttenham, *The Arte of English Poesie*, ed. Gladys D. Willcock and Alice Walker, Cambridge, 1936, pp. 144f.

[15] John Aubrey, *Brief Lives*, ed. Andrew Clark, Oxford, 1898, vol. ii, p. 182.

commonly receiued'.[16] The man born in the wrong part of the country need not worry too much about changing his local vowels, but he must take care to use the right 'terminacions', i.e. the grammatical endings of southern English, and where, in his vocabulary, he had a choice of words, he should take the 'most knowne' word rather than the local dialect form. A few examples taken from a dialogue between master and pupil will illustrate this. The boy is not to write, in imitation of the barbarous speech of his country people, such forms as *stomp* for 'stamp', *hafe* for 'half', *yelk* for 'yolk' (yolk of egg), *suster* for 'sister'. He is told also that a man who lives in the north may write to his neighbour such words as *lathe* for 'barn' and *kirke garth* for 'churchyard', since these are not corruptions of words, but 'if he should write publikely, it is fittest to use the most knowne words'.[17]

Shakespeare's practice, we see, is in full conformity with such precepts. In his dramatic dialogue he is able to capture all the immense variety of the London English of his day, but he makes only moderate use of thieves' English or canting jargon and his plays contain no real dialect parts as such. He is writing for the public stage and can best entertain his audience with a readily comprehensible vocabulary. His dialect speakers have their strong local accents, but they use, in general, 'the most knowne words'. In the play of *Henry V*, we readily understand Fluellen's indignation when the Frenchmen 'Kill the poyes and the luggage' (IV. vii. 1), and he sets the audience the easiest of translation problems in his question 'What call you the Townes name where Alexander the pig was borne?' (IV. vii. 13f.). Edgar, in *King Lear*, speaks in south-western dialect for ten lines or so when he wants to avoid being recognized by the steward Oswald, but the words he uses are almost as plain a language as his blows:

> . . . chill be plaine with you. . . .
> Chill picke your teeth Zir.
>
> (IV. vi. 248, 250)

It is perhaps worth remarking also that the speakers of regional

[16] R.C., *Table Alphabeticall*, 4th ed., 1617, A2v.
[17] Edmund Coote, *The Englishe Schoole-maister*, 1596, p. 31.

dialect in Shakespeare's plays are, so to say, brought into the community, rather than laughed at for being outside it. Edgar, as the 'bold Pezant' stands for rustic virtue. Fluellen the Welshman, Jamy, the Scots captain, and Mackmorrice, the valiant Irish gentleman, vigorously represent the unity of King Henry's force.

How far Shakespeare kept his Warwickshire dialect no one has described for us. As an actor on the London stage he would use, we may suppose, a style of speech that was clear and readily intelligible, as free as possible of local mannerisms. As a playwright, however, Shakespeare is a master of the varied style, and we might well expect that, even in his tragedies, the occasional homely term, from the spoken rather than from the more formal written language, might suit his dramatic purpose. This indeed is what we find. The records of Stratford, of the late sixteenth and early seventeenth century, show a number of what *seem to be* local words which Shakespeare uses in his plays, both in tragedy and comedy. Let me explain what I mean by *seem to be* local. Stratford has a very full collection of town records, many of them written during Shakespeare's lifetime. Some of these have now been printed, some are still to be read in manuscript only. We have, for instance, the accounts of the Chamberlains of the Borough and there are many wills and inventories (these are detailed lists of the goods and chattels of those who died in the town). The student of the Elizabethan language who reads this kind of manuscript local material is bound to find what look like local words, which happen not to have made their way into the printed books of the period, and so have not been registered in the *New English Dictionary*. But it will be readily appreciated that, until there has been a complete survey of the records of every parish and every county, we cannot really know how local such findings are. So far the available records of five or six counties, including Warwickshire, have been searched.

One interesting find at Stratford for the student of Shakespeare's language was in a constable's presentment, i.e. a sworn statement of a suspected offence, undated, but probably *c.* 1627. The phrase 'Aroint thee, witch,' is twice used by Shakespeare, once in *King Lear* (III. iv. 129) and once in *Macbeth* (I. iii. 6), when one of the three witches describes how a sailor's wife refused to give her chestnuts, but cried out instead, 'Aroynt thee, Witch.' This word *aroint* is not found elsewhere in early dialect or proverb or in any work of literature; when Scott uses the phrase in his novel *The Antiquary* (1816) he is obviously imitating Shakespeare. But this constable's presentment of Stratford happens to contain Shakespeare's word and Shakespeare's phrase, when a certain 'goodie bromlie', accused on the very serious charge that she is an 'ill looked' woman, i.e. possessing the evil eye, makes a countercharge, indignantly alleging that it has been said against her:

> . . . I woold over looke her & herne [i.e. her family] as I had over looke others and [she] bid me arent the wich & sayde I was a whore & my bastards mayntayne me & bid me get me hone howe ['one who'] wolld brushe the motes forth of my durtie gowne.

The Stratford record does not, in this instance, give us the meaning of Shakespeare's 'aroint'; this has to be argued from the context and from other evidence. The word seems, in fact, to be a form of 'aloin' from the Anglo-French *aloyner*, so that Shakespeare's phrase has the sense 'Get far away from me'. But in a number of other instances of some importance, knowledge of local usage helps us to a clearer and richer understanding of what Shakespeare's characters are saying in the plays. To cite one brief example: in *Measure for Measure*, when Claudio is led to prison, and is in danger of paying with his life for the offence he has committed, Lucio cheerfully commiserates with him:

> . . . thy head stands so tickle on thy shoulders, that a milke-maid, if she be in loue, may sigh it off. (I. ii. 177ff.)

It seems here that we should expect some joke in the particular connexion which Lucio makes between the *milk*maid and the sighing, and this we find. In a Stratford inventory of 1606 the milkmaid's equipment includes 'on sybolle' [one sye bowl] and one 'milkpan'. And within living memory, it is said, in Shakespeare's country, the 'essential instrument in milking was the see or sye bowl to strain the milk'.[18] Through the language of this Stratford inventory, we understand a further detail of Shakespeare's word-play.

[18] J. H. Bloom, *Folk Lore, Old Customs and Superstitions in Shakespeare Land*, London, 1930, p. 62.

I come next to the question of social dialect in Shakespeare's plays and in the London of his day. The rising prosperity of the lower and middle classes brought with it certain language changes as the newly rich tradesfolk and merchants, proud of the increase in their material wealth, wanted also to rise in the social scale and to give their children, at least, more education and greater cultural advantages. Nashe writes of 'men of obscure parentage . . . equall with Princes in possessions';[19] merchants, we are told elsewhere, bought up the titles of gentlemen and passed off their own children as gentlefolk; complaint is made of low commerce grown rich, while learning is downtrodden. There are many comments on how those who came late in life to wealth and authority tried valiantly, if vainly, to speak with more refinement and dignity. Women, of course, took easily to 'coinesse in gestures . . . minsednesse in woordes and speeches',[20] and the wives of rich merchants are attacked for their affectations. Nashe describes

> Mistris Minx a Marchants wife, that wil eate no Cherries forsooth, but when they are at twenty shillings a pound . . . she is so finicall in her speach, as though she spake nothing but what shee had first sewd over before in her Samplers, and the puling accent of her voyce is like a fained treble, or ones voyce that interprets to the puppets.[21]

But no matter how great the effort of Mistris Minx and her companions, it was only too easy to go wrong: even the word 'forsooth' could serve as a mark of social origin. Ben Jonson shows us that a woman hoping to make her appearance at court was especially cautioned against using the word too often.[22] Falstaff's draper is a 'Rascally-yea-forsooth-knaue' (*2 Hen. IV*, I. ii. 41). Hotspur laughs at his wife for speaking the phrase 'Not mine, in good sooth' (*1 Hen. IV*, III. i. 251ff.):

> You sweare like a Comfit-makers Wife:
> Not you, in good sooth; and, as true as I liue;

[19] Thomas Nashe, *Anatomie of Absurditie*, 1590, D.
[20] Phillip Stubbes, *Anatomie of Abuses*, 1583, G3v.
[21] *Pierce Penilesse, His Supplication to the Diuell*, 1592, B3v.
[22] *Poetaster*, in *Works*, 1616, p. 312.

And, as God shall mend me; and, as sure as day:
And giuest such Sarcenet suretie for thy Oathes,
As if thou neuer walk'st further then Finsbury.
Sweare me, Kate, like a Lady, as thou art,
A good mouth-filling Oath: and leave in sooth,
And such protest of Pepper Ginger-bread,
To Veluet Guards, and Sunday-Citizens.

Where women affect refinement, men affect pomposity. As early as 1553, Thomas Wilson, in the *Arte of Rhetorique*, tells how a good fellow in the country (he seems to have been Dogberry's grandfather)

> beyng an officer, and Maiour of a toune, and desirous to speake like a fine learned man, hauyng iust occasion to rebuke a runnegate felow, said after this wise in a greate heate. Thou yngram and vacacion knaue, if I take thee any more within the circumcision of my dampnacion, I will so corrupte thee, that all vacacion knaues shall take ilsample by thee.

In the discussions on language which continued during the sixteenth and seventeenth centuries, much criticism was directed against the excessive introduction of words of Latin origin. Wilson, while admitting that our language is enriched by some of these borrowings, realizes that not infrequently, as a result of this innovation,

> poore simple men are muche troubled, and talke oftentymes, thei knowe not what, for lacke of wit and want of Latine & Frenche, wherof many of our straunge woordes full often are deriued.[23]

Thirty years later some kinds of mispronunciation had taken root in the class dialect of the lower social group; 'many of the Countrie men', says John Hart (1570), 'speake chalke for cheese' and so nickname the strange new terms which have been brought into the language that 'it pleaseth many well to heare them'.[24] Such men would say, for instance, instead of 'surrender', *sullender* and they would use the mixed form *certisfied* for both 'satisfied' and 'certified'. At this time educated Englishmen were quite seriously watching

[23] *Op. cit.*, fol. 87f.
[24] *A Methode or comfortable beginning for all unlearned, whereby they may bee taught to read English*, A3.

their own speech and writing, so as to get their new words right, i.e. so as to use in customary contexts words already well on the way to acceptance in the language, and it was, no doubt, a very good joke to watch the ignorant getting their new words wrong. From the middle of the sixteenth century many such jokes are used by the playwrights: *Rice pudding cake* is found for 'Respublica';[25] the very word 'ignorant' is changed to *ingram*;[26] 'ransack' becomes *ransackle*;[27] 'stratagem' appears as *sluttegim.*[28] Some of the fun of Shakespeare's early plays comes from this 'derangement of epitaphs'. In *A Midsummer Night's Dream* Bottom welcomes Quince's suggestion that they shall meet 'in the palace wood, a mile without the Towne, by Moone-light'. There, says Bottom, 'we may rehearse more obscenely and couragiously' (I. ii. 111). Launce in *The Two Gentlemen of Verona* has received his 'proportion, like the prodigious Sonne' (II. iii. 4). Dogberry's part in *Much Ado* is written almost wholly in this type of language, but even here, in using the convention, Shakespeare contrives to go beyond it. There can never have been a richer compression of meaning than we hear in Dogberry's dictum that 'Comparisons are odorous' (III. v. 18). Malapropism in such characters, it has been pointed out, 'is not a mere stage trick; it rests upon a difference in literacy between those days and these. . . . It is the inevitable result of hearing long words and never seeing them.'[29]

Pedants and scholars who had heard and seen too many long words, who had, in the words of the Curate in *Love's Labour's Lost* (IV. ii. 26f.), 'eate paper' and 'drunke inke', and whose English talk, in consequence, was overloaded with Latinisms, provide another source of enjoyment in the Elizabethan theatre. For well over half a century there was vigorous and serious controversy over the amount of Latin that could properly be absorbed into the English language. One writer, in 1586, makes energetic protest that if the Latin borrowings of the last few years:

[25] *Respublica,* ed. by W. W. Greg, 1952, p. 22.

[26] *Three Lords and Three Ladies of London*, 1590, C1v.

[27] Ben Jonson, *A Tale of a Tub*, 1640, p. 92.

[28] *Two Wise Men and All the Rest Fools* (1619), Tudor Facsimile Texts, 1913, p. 23.

[29] Gladys D. Willcock, 'Shakespeare and Elizabethan English', *A Companion to Shakespeare Studies*, ed. by H. Granville-Barker and G. B. Harrison, Cambridge, 1934, p. 130.

> should be all counted inkpot tearmes, I know not how we should speak anie thing without blacking our mouths with inke; for what word can be more plain than this word (plaine) & yet what can come more neere to the Latine? What more manifest than (manifest)? & yet in a manner Latine: What more commune than (rare), or lesse rare than (commune) & yet both of them comming of the Latine? But you will saie, long vse hath made these wordes currant: and why may not vse doe as much for these wordes which we shall now deriue?[30]

Puttenham, three years later, attacks the affectations of the over-learned; he describes it as an 'intollerable ill maner of speach . . . when we affect new words and phrases other then the good speakers and writers in any language, or then custome hath allowed'.[31] He finds this is a common fault in young scholars 'not halfe well studied', who, when they leave the university and the schools and happen to get some benefice or other promotion in the country, 'will seeme to coigne fine wordes out of the Latin, and to vse new fangled speaches thereby to shew themselues among the ignorant the better learned'. Elsewhere he speaks of the 'many inkhorne termes so ill affected brought in by men of learning as preachers and schoole-masters'.[32] In *Love's Labour's Lost* Shakespeare has much delightful satire on such men of learning. What 'the rude multitude call the after-noone' Armado, the fantastical Spaniard, designates as 'the posteriors of this day' (V. i. 94ff.). The schoolmaster Holofernes applauds his word as 'liable, congruent, and measurable'.

The question of Shakespeare's own 'smalle Latine and lesse Greeke' is best settled by reference to his writings. As Professor T. W. Baldwin has very thoroughly demonstrated, even though there is 'no direct evidence that he ever attended any grammar school a single day' he shows in his plays and poems a mastery of all such knowledge and techniques as grammar school was calculated to give.[33] It is important to remember also that all lessons had to be committed to memory, so that whatever knowledge Shakespeare and his educated contemporaries got in their grammar schooling

[30] *The ciuile Conuersation of M. Stephen Guazzo*, trans. George Pettie. (I quote from Pettie's address to his reader.)

[31] G. Puttenham, *Arte of English Poesie*, p. 251f.

[32] *Ibid.*, p. 145.

[33] T. W. Baldwin, *William Shakspere's Small Latine And Lesse Greek*, Urbana, 1944, vol. ii, p. 662.

they 'would have so long as memory did last'.[34] For dramatist and for many of his audience a knowledge of Latin was in grain, part of the material of mental growth. And we shall better understand what was in the Shakespearian text for the eyes and ears of his contemporaries the more we can become responsive to the Latin-English language patterns which were fixed for life in the average Elizabethan mind. We can, for example, by reference to the Latin dictionaries of Shakespeare's time, understand, without the drastic surgery of emendation, some of the longstanding difficulties of the dramatic dialogue. In Othello's phrase 'my defunct, and proper satisfaction' (*Othello*, I. iii. 265) the word *defunct* is seen to mean 'free of danger, punishment, penalty incurred'. Sometimes our understanding of the wit of a comic passage depends on a knowledge of Latin idiom. I take here one brief example, a joke sparked off in passing as Celia talks with Touchstone the jester in *As You Like It* (I. ii. 89ff.). Touchstone speaks to Celia in a rather disparaging way about the honour of one of the knights whom her father loves, and Celia cuts him short with the rebuke:

> My Fathers loue is enough to honor him enough; speake no more of him, you'l be whipt for taxation one of these daies.

'Taxation' can mean 'accusation': Touchstone will be whipped, says Celia, for making slanderous charges. But some of Shakespeare's audience would hear, no doubt, a second sense in the *whipt/taxation* connexion. The Latin 'tax' has the meaning 'the sound of a stroke with a whip'.

I come next to the sound barrier, the differences in language between Shakespeare's world and our own, and shall speak of changes in vocabulary and idiom which prevent us from bringing to the Shakespearian play the intent and living responsiveness of the Elizabethan audience. It sometimes seems quite strange that, four hundred years after the birth of England's greatest dramatist, there should still be many questions to be asked and answered on the basic problem of what the words mean in his text. One major difficulty is, of course, that the language of a play is essentially something spoken and something heard; the meaning of the words is not static. In the swift

[34] Baldwin, *op. cit.*, vol. i, p. 197.

interchange of comic dialogue the speakers may seem like clever jugglers, tossing into the air the several senses of the single word and changing the ranges of meaning with effortless skill. Personal tragedy may turn old idiom to new application; a sense of the complexity of life may lead to complexity of language; in Hamlet's claim to 'know a Hawke from a Handsaw' (II. ii. 397), there is a unique compression of several meanings—the falconer's 'sore' is a hawk of the first year that has not moulted and still has the red plumage. We should have in mind also that with an audience trained to strenuous listening and quick response it might even be useful to the playwright occasionally to hold up the speed of that response. He might choose to write what would be, momentarily, unintelligible; might, of deliberate intent, block the way forward, compel the hearer to pause before taking in. Both in comedy and tragedy there could be profit for the playwright in an emphasis so achieved.[35]

The problem is made more difficult by the fact that we do not know nearly enough of the ordinary spoken language of Shakespeare's world. Colloquial language has always, as it were, its shorthand symbols; quotation fragments from larger language groupings bring with them their own contexts; those inside the community hear in full what is spoken in part. Within the Elizabethan language group, the quotation fragment *three sleeves* implied stealing. The later student needs the saying in full: The tailor cuts three sleeves for every woman's gown, i.e. he asks for more material than is required. Shakespeare makes play with this joke through an emphasized '*two* sleeues' in *The Taming of the Shrew* (IV. iii. 142). Another fragment of idiom *to pay sauce* means 'to be overcharged'; in its full form the saying is to find the sauce worse than the meat, i.e. to discover too late that the trimmings cost more than the main dish. Sometimes, too, the Elizabethan idiom has changed its form in later language. Where we get the *sack*, Shakespeare's contemporaries would be given the *bag*. The Elizabethan idiom is the more difficult for us to understand since our own *sack* in this sense seems never to have held our luggage.

The last difficulty I shall mention is that of being sensitive to the wrong idiom patterns, of having non-Elizabethan prejudgements

[35] Hilda M. Hulme, *Explorations in Shakespeare's language*, London, 1962, p. 6.

and associations. For although it is true that the early printed texts of Shakespeare's plays undoubtedly contain some errors which may have been introduced by copyist or printer, yet, not infrequently, even at the present time, the Shakespearian editor, seeking to restore what Shakespeare wrote, is, in fact, rewriting Shakespeare's words so as to make them conform to the language expectations of a later day. I cite first two merely cautionary tales. Where, as I quoted earlier, Regan says to her father in *King Lear*, 'I pray you Father being weake, seeme so' (II. iv. 204), an eighteenth century-editor, some of whose emendations are still accepted, proposed the correction, 'I pray you, father, being 'wake, seem so'.[36] Where Lady Macbeth speaks the lines,

> Nor Heauen peepe through the Blanket of the darke
> To cry, hold, hold . . .
>
> (I. v. 54f.)

Coleridge at one time suspected that Shakespeare had written 'blank height' of the dark; for this he gave classical authority.[37] And in a modern text of *Macbeth* (I. iii. 97f.), when messages of Macbeth's victories are brought in quick succession to King Duncan, we usually find the image 'As thick as hail Came post with post'. This word *hail* was introduced by an early eighteenth-century editor;[38] but we ought, I think, to remember that what comes thick as hail, we would like to find shelter against; messages of victory do not come 'thick as hail'. The original text of 1623 has the image 'as thick as Tale', which sounds to modern ears, of course, quite ludicrous; only a 'tail' is 'thick' in present-day English. But the Elizabethan and early seventeenth-century 'tale' has the normal meaning 'talk'. And if we examine the various 'talking' idioms in which *tale*, *thick* and *post* are found at this time, and then apply this information to the original Shakespearian text, we find that the messengers came in quick succession, fast as the spoken word.

Shakespeare's language lives in the demands it makes upon our alertness. And I end now with the words of Heminge and Condell, Shakespeare's first editors, his friends and fellow actors:

> Reade him, therefore; and againe, and againe.

[36] Sir Thomas Hanmer, 1745.
[37] *Coleridge's: Shakespearean Criticism*, ed. by T. M. Raysor, 1960, vol. i, p. 65.
[38] Nicholas Rowe, 1709.

VIII

The Course of Shakespeare Criticism

T. J. B. SPENCER

In considering Shakespeare and his critics, we can begin at the beginning. For a poet's first critic is the self-critic. What did Shakespeare think of his own writings? He failed to provide us with his literary memoirs; we lack anything like Ben Jonson's literary notebooks, or that ironical poem of Lope de Vega on the art of writing stage plays, or the *Dichtung und Wahrheit* of Goethe. But Shakespeare wrote more than a million words; and we might expect to be able to deduce from them something of his attitudes to his own art.

Literary criticism was not very expressive in his time; not expressive about the literature actually being written, especially the popular drama. Shakespeare's most lengthy and serious piece of criticism concerns not the art of poetry or the art of drama, but the art of acting. As a full-time professional man of the theatre, he was perhaps most deeply concerned with the techniques of his own profession. The famous passage is memorable not so much for its content or meaning as for its sophistication.

> Let your own discretion be your tutor: suit the action to the word, the word to the action; with this special observance, that you o'erstep not the modesty of nature; for anything so overdone is from the purpose of playing, whose end, both at the first and now, was and is, to hold, as 'twere, the mirror up to nature; to show virtue her own feature, scorn her own image, and the very age and body of the time his form and pressure. Now, this overdone, or come tardy off, though it make the unskilful laugh, cannot but make the judicious grieve; the censure of the which one must in your allowance o'erweigh a whole theatre of others. (*Hamlet*, III. ii. 18ff.)

There is nothing comparable to this among Shakespeare's discussions of literature. Perhaps, like many actors and dramatists, he was not favourable to literary critics. His one detailed representation of a character of this kind is distinctly harsh. This literary critic is finicky about particular words and phrases, giving his commendation or censure merely according to his taste; he is easily bored; he prattles about nature and art in a vague, theoretical way; he has formulas for the particular 'genres' or kinds of plays, and is a judge of figures of speech. He is keen on the classical background; and his experience of the drama—an honour he does not forget—is that he was long ago the leading member of his college amateur dramatic society.

As a literary critic Polonius is shown as scarcely capable of seeing beyond his beard.

Polonius. My liege, and madam, to expostulate
What majesty should be, what duty is,
Why day is day, night night, and time is time,
Were nothing but to waste night, day, and time.
Therefore, since brevity is the soul of wit,
And tediousness the limbs and outward flourishes,
I will be brief. Your noble son is mad:
Mad call I it: for, to define true madness,
What is't but to be nothing else but mad?
But let that go.
Queen. More matter, with less art.
Polonius. Madam, I swear I use no art at all.

(II. ii. 86ff.)

It is difficult not to remember Ben Jonson's postprandial and perhaps bibulous conversations with William Drummond long afterwards and the curt statement that 'Shakespeare wanted art'. Was this a private joke in the Company? (*Hamlet* has an unusual amount of theatre-gossip in it.) And perhaps the writer of the Latin epitaph on Shakespeare's monument in the parish church of Stratford on Avon wanted to do something to scotch the story of Shakespeare's lack of art, and so endowed his fellow citizen with

Judicio Pylium, genio Socratem, *arte* Maronem.

Meanwhile Polonius becomes entangled in the arts of language.

> That he is mad, 'tis true; 'tis true, 'tis pity;
> And pity 'tis, 'tis true: a foolish figure;
> But farewell it, for I will use no art.

This insistence seems to be breaking the wind of the poor jest, especially as Polonius is still inextricable from verbal art:

> Mad let us grant him, then; and now remains
> That we find out the cause of this effect,
> Or rather say, the cause of this defect,
> For this effect defective comes by cause;
> Thus it remains, and the remainder thus.
> Perpend.
>
> (II. ii. 97ff.)

Polonius's efforts at verbal criticism are on the same level: ' "beautified" is a vile phrase', but ' "mobled queen" is good'. Although he prattles about nature and art, and matter and art, yet he believes in inspiration:

> How pregnant sometimes his replies are! a happiness that often madness hits on, which reason and sanity could not so prosperously be delivered of. (II. ii. 212ff.)

Polonius's introduction of the company of travelling players cannot be other than a joke at the Renaissance categorization of the drama and at the failure of the theorists to accommodate the plays actually successful on the popular stage:

> The best actors in the world, either for tragedy, comedy, history, pastoral, pastoral-comical, historical-pastoral, tragical-historical, tragical-comical-historical-pastoral, scene individable, or poem unlimited: Seneca cannot be too heavy, nor Plautus too light. For the law of writ and the liberty, these are the only men. (II. ii. 415ff.)

When he 'played once i' the university', he was (Polonius himself states) 'accounted a good actor'. He played the leading role: 'I did enact Julius Caesar: I was kill'd in the Capitol; Brutus killed me' (III. ii. 104). On the strength of this amateur experience he takes it upon himself to judge Hamlet's ability as an actor: ''Fore God, my lord, well spoken; with good accent and good discretion' (II. ii. 488). But Hamlet disables his judgement, in the presence of the players:

'Prithee, say on. He's for a jig or a tale of bawdry, or he sleeps' (II. ii. 522).

All this, surely, shows a sophisticated attitude to literature. And the impression is confirmed by other passages in the plays and poems. It is not of much significance that the word *critical* is first recorded in Shakespeare ('That is some satire, keen and critical': *A Midsummer Night's Dream*, V. i. 54), because the meaning is, presumably, merely 'censorious'. Of more interest, it seems, is the fact that Shakespeare usually put his ideas on literature into a comic or ironic context or situation. Sir Philip Sidney had praised the virtue of poetical 'sincerity' in *The Apologie for Poetrie*, and had permitted his Muse to instruct him in the initial sonnet of *Astrophel and Stella*: 'Look in thy heart and write.' And perhaps Shakespeare had, for the purposes of entertainment, acceded to the notion in Berowne's speech in *Love's Labour's Lost*:

> Never durst poet touch a pen to write
> Until his ink were temper'd with Love's sighs (IV. iii. 346f.)

But Touchstone had other views when talking to his Audrey:

> When a man's verses cannot be understood, nor a man's good wit seconded with the forward child Understanding, it strikes a man more dead than a great reckoning in a little room. Truly, I would the gods had made thee poetical.
> *Audrey*. I do not know what 'poetical' is. Is it honest in deed and word? Is it a true thing?
> *Touchstone*. No, truly, for the truest poetry is the most feigning; and lovers are given to poetry, and what they swear in poetry may be said as lovers they do feign.
> *Audrey*. Do you wish then that the gods had made me poetical?
> *Touchstone*. I do, truly; for thou swearest to me thou art honest: now, if thou wert a poet, I might have some hope thou didst feign.
> (*As You Like It*, III. iii. 12ff.)

We observe the comment on theories of poetical inspiration: 'I would *the gods* had made thee poetical.' This reminds us of Theseus's somewhat disparaging remark about 'the poet's eye, in a fine *frenzy* rolling' (*A Midsummer Night's Dream*, V. i. 12). The association of the poet with the lunatic and the lover ('of imagination all compact') is hardly an encouraging comment on the doctrine of *furor poeticus*.

There are also plenty of jokes on poetry and poets. Hotspur, the man of action, had rather be a kitten and cry mew. And (perhaps most interesting of all) the poet in *Timon of Athens* is cunningly drawn: a combination of false modesty, self-centredness, and verbal flow: an unflattering picture of the professional men-of-letters, whom Shakespeare must sometimes have met—not the professional theatre-men like Shakespeare, but the professionals who stood up for the dignity of literature; perhaps that rival poet with 'the proud full sail of his great verse', he who drew inspiration from

> that affable familiar ghost,
> Which nightly gulls him with intelligence. (Sonnet 86.)

—all those who wrote to be read, and who disparaged stage plays even though they condescended to employ their pens on them.

Shakespeare clearly made a great impression on his contemporaries. But, in fact, he had not been regarded as unique. Those who had praised him *had* naturally praised him in relation to other writers of his time (Spenser, Sidney, Chapman, Jonson, Fletcher . . .), and therefore some of the praise (for instance, that of Webster in his preface to *The White Devil*) may sound rather condescending. But in the seventeenth century (until Dryden) his admirers were not able to decide and define exactly what the impression was. Shakespeare was a lively and fluent writer; of great fancy and versatility; sweetness and strength; also diligent and productive. But the careful collections that have been made of references to Shakespeare in the seventeenth century show how many writers did *not* mention Shakespeare or paid little attention to him. The superior reputation of Ben Jonson, for the first half of the century at least, is explicable. Ben Jonson was manifestly a *writer*. He produced *literature*. He published his *Works* (1616). He was a man of intellectual authority, a scholar and a philosopher, with qualities making him seem important to the young and pretentious. Ben Jonson was, moreover, the most vocal literary critic of the early seventeenth century, and found Shakespeare convenient—a contrast to himself, for the purposes of that rough-and-ready synthesis or miscellany of Renaissance theorizing which Jonson compiled or 'conveyed'. He gave Shakespeare a kind of typological significance—the naturally gifted writer who fails to discipline himself. He turned Shakespeare into a kind of sparring partner or stooge, which he could use in order to justify his own rather solemn and laborious critical position.

Of course, in contrasting himself with Shakespeare, Jonson saw something that was really there. But from Jonson derived the commonplace about Nature and Art, which (we must admit) for long proved to be a pertinacious and unproductive theme of Shakespeare criticism. It was picked up by Milton in his thoughtless youth, when he complimented Shakespeare:

> to the shame of slow-endeavouring art
> Thy easy numbers flow . . .

When a great literary genius appears he has to be explained in terms of the current literary ideas. His similarities to these are noticed, as in the case of Ben Jonson; or the differences, as in the case of Shakespeare. The notion of Shakespeare as a natural genius who did not fit into Renaissance notions of artistry was further encouraged by Milton, when he contrasted Jonson's 'learned sock' with Shakespeare's 'native woodnotes wild' (which refers to the comedies, but came to be treated as a general statement, especially the epithet 'wild'). A good deal of the spirit of Ben Jonson's cavillings, rather than his magnificent praise in the poem prefixed to the Folio of 1623, was continued by the later seventeenth- and eighteenth-century critics, censuring Shakespeare's carelessness, his notorious artistic 'faults'.

Dryden was concerned with his own art as a dramatist, and he judged Shakespeare in a practical spirit. For the next hundred years the best literary criticism of Shakespeare can be seen to be an elaboration and clarification of Dryden's opinions. Dryden on some occasions praised Shakespeare in the highest terms: 'the man who of all modern, and perhaps ancient poets, had the largest and most comprehensive soul'.[1]

But as we all know, in spite of this praise, Dryden exercised his talents in making versions of the plays which were better adapted to the taste of the theatre after the Restoration of King Charles II; and,

[1] *Essays of John Dryden*, ed. W. P. Ker, vol. i, p. 79 ('An Essay of Dramatic Poesy').

in fact, there is some inconsistency in Dryden's expression of his opinions. At times he attributes artistic 'faults' to Shakespeare, judging him according to the neo-classical principles of taste which were soon prevailing throughout Europe. Shakespeare's dramatic art was so different from that of the admired tragedy of the times (that of Corneille and Racine) that it was difficult to defend or interpret it in reasonable terms. Shakespeare was felt to have little sense of aesthetic decorum: this was proved especially by his marring tragic feeling in his plays by comic intrusions. Secondly, he was incorrigibly careless and ridiculously ignorant about matters of fact; his frequent anachronisms, however trivial in themselves, disturbed and disconcerted the reader's imagination. Thirdly, he displayed fundamental defects of style, which reveal themselves in puns and senseless quibbles, images ludicrously mixed, offending and defying all canons of good writing. These defects of Shakespeare were perceived more by readers than by playgoers; the theatrical versions of the plays generally included revisions in accordance with the new principles of taste. The continued and increasing popularity of Shakespeare on the stage from 1660 and throughout the eighteenth century undermined the influence of neo-classical censure of his 'faults'. The playgoers, for whom the 'impression' from the play was the test of its worth, instinctively accepted (for the most part) Shakespeare's artistry, while the literary critics doubted it.

In the early eighteenth century the cumbrous folios (1623, 1632, 1663, 1685) were replaced by more convenient editions, prepared for the reader. Rowe in his six-volume edition of 1709 tidied up the text of the plays, adding scene divisions, lists of dramatis personae, indications of locality, and so on. The importance of this for criticism is not to be neglected; for hitherto Shakespeare's plays had been either expendable play-books or heavy folios. But though Rowe thus turned Shakespeare's plays into literature to be read, he was himself a practising and successful dramatist and on the whole he gave an excellent lead to the dramatic criticism of the plays. His example was not followed by Alexander Pope the poet, whose preface to his edition in 1725 had an unhappy influence on criticism. Shakespeare, according to Pope, was a great natural genius—his skill of characterization was excellent; he exercised a power over one's feelings, and he had great gifts of lively expression. His artistic defects were great, but they were not altogether his own fault. He wrote to please 'the meaner sort of people', without the patronage of the educated upper classes; and so he marred his tragedies by the comic intrusions of the lower orders. He himself was an actor, and his companions were actors ('the worst of company', said Pope). His plays were given to the press by two actors (Heminge and Condell) and they used the prompter's copies in which the texts were contaminated by additions for clowns, by confusions of speeches (due to the doubling of parts in productions), by the shuffling of scenes and transferring of speeches (due to actors' jealousies), and by the insertion of bombastic speeches for the use of ranting actors; it is wonderful that Shakespeare's natural genius could shine through in spite of all his disadvantages. Pope thus fully accepts the artistic form of Shakespeare's writings as due to their being stage-plays; but he regards this fact as their main disadvantage and the source of their artistic defectiveness.

Broadly seen, the history of Shakespeare criticism from the time of Pope consists of four phases. First, Shakespeare was the poet born, one who without self-conscious art or formal education created masterpieces by instinct. The plays, excellent though they were, had to be revised by more skilful hands for the modern theatre. During this period the predominant literary form was the drama, though, to be sure, great plays were few. This is the Shakespeare of Rowe, Pope, Lord Chesterfield, and Hume; and (expressed with the subtle discriminations of a great critic) it is the Shakespeare of Dr. Johnson.

During the first decades of the nineteenth century (and before that, in Germany) this attitude to Shakespeare had become incredible and repellent. His artistry was now seen to be 'unconscious' or 'organic'. The dominant literary forms were those of self-revelatory poetry. Hamlet was felt to speak with the voice and feeling of Shakespeare, and, as for the *Sonnets*, Wordsworth, whose greatest achievement was writing a long poem on the growth of his own mind, explained to an already convinced world that 'with this key Shakespeare unlocked his heart'. His writings were the allegory of the human soul. The Shakespeare of Goethe and Schlegel was the Shakespeare of Coleridge and Keats, and (belatedly) of Victor Hugo and Taine, and of Belinsky.

These critical methods of the early nineteenth century were inclined to degenerate in inferior hands in the course of the century: the belief in Shakespeare's all-pervading artistry led to oversubtle interpretations; the enthusiasm for character-analysis led to biography-writing in a novelistic rather than a strictly dramatic framework; and the acknowledged assessment of Shakespeare's keen intelligence led to his being associated with almost every school of thought in religion, politics, morals, psychology, and metaphysics. Nevertheless, it was the great achievement of the early nineteenth century critics to have got away from the discussion of 'beauties' and 'faults' in Shakespeare and to enable criticism to devote itself to interpreting the delight which people had always felt in the plays, whether as readers or theatre goers. They sought for new subtleties and new excellences; and it became an achievement in literary criticism to have found an explanation for some hitherto difficult or irreconcilable detail in a play. Shakespeare's 'faults' now became problems. Many of the most brilliant writers of Europe were critics of Shakespeare; and their utterances are notable as recording the impressions he made upon great minds.

There is a kind of typology of poets. Each age, looking back upon the great literary figures of the past, finds it difficult to avoid making them conform to its own characteristic idea of The Poet. Sometimes there may exist more than one pattern; or rather, alongside the dominant pattern, there may exist survivals of the typology of the last age and anticipations of the next. In the nineteenth century the vision of Shakespeare was twofold. He was seen as the romantic poet (of which Byron was the European type), and as the poetical sage (for which an elderly view of Goethe, Tennyson, or Browning will serve). These were not really inconsistent. Indeed, ingenuity could be exercised in showing how consistent they were. For it seemed obvious that, had not Byron heroically died young, he would eventually have ripened into a poetical sage like Goethe.

The Byronic Shakespeare, even if he eventually capitulated to the Olympian Shakespeare, was for long tenaciously preserved in the fancy. A prim Englishman could write about Shakespeare in a popular history of English literature: 'It is more than probable that his education was neglected, his passions strong, and his conduct far from regular.'[2] But a Frenchman, who saw Shakespeare as the giant forerunner of his own romantic men of letters, described him with more excitement and vivacity; to Hippolyte Taine, Shakespeare was

> a man of almost superhuman passions, extreme in joy and grief, agitated and impetuous in his transports, with passions as precocious as they were imprudent, conscience-less, but sensitive to every touch of pleasure, a man of inordinate and extravagant genius.[3]

The approximation of Shakespeare to the Byronic type of poet had a remarkable manifestation in the popularity of Shakespeare's physical infirmity. It was interesting to observe that, like Lord Byron himself and Sir Walter Scott, as well as the Prayers in Homer who followed behind Sin, Shakespeare suffered from lameness. This had, of course, been noted already in the eighteenth century, though the suggestion made no appeal to the pedestrian mind of Malone, and was rejected by him.[4] But the evidence was striking. In Sonnet 89 Shakespeare wrote:

> Say that thou did'st forsake me for some fault,
> And I will comment upon that offence;
> *Speak of my lameness, and I straight will halt,*
> Against thy reasons making no defence.

This was a curious statement, but hardly conclusive. Again, in Sonnet 37, he wrote:

> As a decrepit father takes delight
> To see his active child do deeds of youth,
> So I, *made lame by fortune's dearest spite,*
> Take all my comfort of thy word and truth.

It is clear that the *lame* and *lameness* could, in both these instances, be taken in a metaphorical sense. But unhappily Sonnet 37 continues:

> For whether beauty, birth, or wealth, or wit,
> Or any of these all, or all, or more,
> Entitled in thy parts do crowned sit,
> I make my love engrafted to this store:
> *So then I am not lame, poor, nor despised,*
> Whilst that this shadow doth such substance give . . .

[2] Thomas Budd Shaw, *A History of English Literature,* ed. William Smith (1864), p. 137.

[3] *Histoire de la littérature anglaise* (1864), book II, ch. iv.

[4] By Capell in a note on Sonnets 37 and 38. 1821 Variorum, vol. xx, p. 26.

Here *lame* means something distinct from *poor* or *despised*. It really seemed to have a literal meaning. And there was corroborative evidence. Although no mention of the defect in Shakespeare's legs (which would have been so obvious on the stage) was made by his contemporaries, yet the only parts which he is believed to have himself performed as an actor were those of old men. Perhaps it was owing to his lameness that he was employed on the stage only to represent the decrepit or such parts as were compatible with his measured and impeded locomotion, such as Old Knowell in *Every Man in His Humour*, the ghost in *Hamlet*, and Adam in *As You Like It*. Indeed, the tradition of his having taken the part of old Adam was particularly interesting; for Orlando refers to his faithful servitor in terms appropriate:

> There is an old poor man,
> Who after me hath many a weary step
> *Limp'd* in pure love.
>
> (II. vii. 129ff.)

Of course, even if Shakespeare had been lame, it clearly did not disqualify him from active bodily exertion. Sonnets 50 and 51 show that he was a horseman. Sir Walter Scott introduced Shakespeare into *Kenilworth* as a comrade in lameness, but a vigorous one. There, the Earl of Sussex describes the young poet to Queen Elizabeth.

> He is a stout man at quarter-staff, and single falchion, though, as I am told, a halting fellow; and he stood, they say, a tough fight with the rangers of old Sir Thomas Lucy of Charlecot, when he broke his deer-park and kissed his keeper's daughter (Chapter xvii).

(This was one of Scott's anachronisms, for in 1575, the date of Queen Elizabeth's visit to Kenilworth, Shakespeare was only eleven years old.) Another warm supporter of Shakespeare's lameness was William Harness, a schoolfellow of Byron and himself lame. Malone's argument for rejecting Capell's suggestion was based on the line, 'Speak of my lameness, and I straight will halt', where he remarked that 'if Shakespeare was in truth lame, he had it not in his power to *halt occasionally* for this or any other purpose. The defect must have been fixed and permanent.' Not so, cried Harness.

> Surely, many an infirmity of the kind may be skilfully concealed; or

> only become visible in the moments of hurried movement. Either Sir Walter Scott or Lord Byron might, without any impropriety, have written the verses in question. They would have been applicable to either of them. Indeed, the lameness of Lord Byron was exactly such as Shakespeare's might have been; and I remember as a boy that he selected those speeches for declamation which would not constrain him to the use of such exertions as might obtrude the defect of his person into notice..[5]

When William Harness visited Stratford in 1844 he kept a journal which has recently been published.[6]

> As I took the short cut over the fields to Shottery this morning I am as satisfied that I was not only looking to the same hill as he would have had before his eyes, but that I was treading the very path to what was the house of the Hathaways which he would have trod, as if I had seen him hurrying on before me, the limp in his gait become more conspicuous than it was in general from the rapid movement to which he was urged by his impatience to reach his love.

At the time when Scott and Byron were the two literary lions of London, Hookham Frere remarked: 'Great poets formerly were blind' (thinking of Homer and Milton): 'now they are lame.'[7]

But in one respect Shakespeare's attitude to his lameness was very different from Childe Harold's; he was far from being ashamed of his infirmity. He was not afraid, Chateaubriand pointed out,[8] even of reminding one of his mistresses about it in sonnets he addressed to her. How unlike Byron's secretiveness on the subject!

So it seemed probable that the cause of Shakespeare's lameness was not to be sought in anything discreditable. One of the persuasively argued theories in Victorian England was that Shakespeare had spent some time as a soldier in the Netherlands; his infirmity may have been due to an accident during his military service, even possibly in battle-action. If he had acquired it honourably, that would explain his lack of reticence on the subject.[9]

But gradually this romantic item of Shakespeare's personal

[5] 'Life of Shakespeare', prefixed to his edition of *The Dramatic Works* (8 vols., 1825), p. xliii.

[6] *Shakespeare Survey*, vol. xiv (1961), pp. 110ff.

[7] *The Table-Talk of Samuel Rogers*, ed. Alexander Dyce (1856), p. 192.

[8] *Essai sur la littérature anglaise* (1836), p. 282.

[9] W. J. Thoms in *Notes and Queries*, 1859 (2nd series, vii, 333ff. and 351ff.); reprinted in *Three Notelets on Shakespeare* (1865).

appearance fell into disrepute; and when Swinburne wrote his mocking 'Report of the Proceedings on the First Anniversary Session of the Newest Shakespeare Society' (a burlesque of the activities of the New Shakspere Society which Furnivall had founded in 1874), he introduced a member as reading a paper on 'The Lameness of Shakespeare—was it moral or physical?'[10] It is soon concluded that the infirmity was physical. Then arose the question—in which leg? The lecturer was prepared, on the evidence of a passage in *The Two Gentlemen of Verona*, to demonstrate that the injured and interesting limb was the left one, not the right one. 'This shoe is my father,' says Launce. 'No, this left shoe is my father; no, no, this left shoe is my mother: nay, that cannot be so neither: yes, it is so, it is so, *it hath the worser sole*.' (II. iii. 16.) Launce's remarks were not necessary either to the progress of the play or to the development of the character; and so it was a reasonable inference that, without some personal allusion, they must have been as unintelligible to the audience as they had hitherto been to the commentators. We need not continue with Swinburne's interpretation of 'made lame by Fortune's dearest spite' as an allusion to an accident which befell Shakespeare in early life when he was acting at the Fortune Theatre. Alas, Shakespeare's romantic and Byronic lameness had degenerated into nothing more than an object of Swinburne's fun.

It is a common enough remark that each age sees what it wants to see in Shakespeare; that each age sees itself in Shakespeare; that Shakespeare criticism will change as the world changes. But we need to give some sense of reality and significance to this customary remark. The identification of Shakespeare with the most vital intellectual interests of the time gives Shakespeare criticism vivacity and intensity; it distinguishes criticism from uncritical scholarship. We must feel we are fighting for the real Shakespeare. However often the sceptic and relativist may say that we shall only see what we can and that we can only see what we must, and however deeply we may be embedded in the 'situation', yet great criticism, like all intellectual feats, is a leaping out of the 'situation'. And the history of Shakespeare criticism is a cautionary tale, a warning against an insolent

[10] First published in *The Examiner*, 1 April 1876, it was reprinted as an appendix to *A Study of Shakespeare* (1880), pp. 284–5.

view of criticism as a steadily progressing pursuit of truth. It is easy enough to be amused by the follies and preoccupations of the past. Few of those who write about the history of Shakespeare criticism can resist the temptation to be funny about it, though they ought to rise to the dignity of the theme. We, too, need a good-humoured awareness of the kinds of bias which deflect our minds nowadays.

The story of Shakespeare's lameness may be read as a parable of Shakespeare criticism; a moral and an application can be extracted for the benefit of critics during the last hundred and fifty years. Shakespeare certainly became a kind of Victorian sage, a realist and a moralizer; one who was wise in his generation; who saw life steadily; the voice of England, and the protector of the proprieties, and the prophet of the New Woman; one who had graduated in the university of life; the self-made man with a soul, as was revealed in the standard biographies of Halliwell-Phillipps and Sidney Lee. The dominant literary form had come to be the moralizing novel, and it was natural for the critics to fall into the habit of reading the plays with something of the attitude of mind they brought to George Eliot.

The literature of the twentieth century belongs to a post-symbolist world, with peculiar and autonomous literary values. The great literary work is expected to reveal, perhaps in a fragmentary and oblique form, something of the human condition, the predicament of modern man, with outcroppings, perhaps, of the *philosophia perennis*; preserving a certain Christian (at least, traditional) stability in a humanistic world in which all coherence is going. It is the world of *Ulysses* and *The Waste Land* (rather than *Middlemarch* or *The Doll's House*). Not forgetting the parable of Shakespeare's lameness, we can perhaps discern in what ways assumptions about the nature of poets and poetry are guiding our perceptions and understanding of Shakespeare. We may perhaps conveniently consider, in this fourth phase of Shakespeare criticism, the post-Victorian moralists.

No great poet has made it so difficult for posterity to gain a clear and reliable notion of his moral nature and his views on the human condition as has Shakespeare; and in the case of no poet is curiosity regarding these matters so intense. The meagre information regarding his domestic and emotional history is tantalizing. But when presented with a bulk of writing consisting of over a million words, it is impossible to complain about the scarcity of evidence for ascertaining Shakespeare's views on Life. To discover a new fact about his marriage or the progress of his lawsuits demands patient labour among tedious and scarcely legible archives. To discourse on his knowledge of music, theology, ornithology, comets, lunacy, or the Ottoman Empire, must be left to the experts in those subjects. But we are all expert moralists. It requires no special knowledge or professional training to expound the relation between Shakespeare and Life. The plays are there to be read; and it is a natural impulse delightedly to discover, and to reveal to the world, that Shakespeare was as wise and perceptive as ourselves.

Again, it is generally believed that the practice of writing, at least of writing well, is in some way related to a just perception of human values. Although we may discount the long tradition of moral exhortation in literature, we should find it hard to abandon the notion that the creative writer can in some way grasp the significance of human life—without, of course, necessarily giving us any positive instructions how to behave ourselves. It was some time before the study of Shakespeare succumbed to this very reasonable prejudice. Dr. Johnson had sternly reprimanded Shakespeare: 'He sacrifices virtue to convenience, and is so much more careful to please than to instruct, that he seems to write without any moral purpose.' But the German critics of the nineteenth century changed all that, and discerned in his plays something more than a repository of worldly wisdom and shrewd empirical observation of mankind. There was a moral profundity more important than that: a deep *poetical* insight into human nature, into life itself. In each play could be discerned certain essential themes or fundamental ideas, revealed or perhaps concealed, directly or symbolically, by the action. It was a hardy doctrine, which has survived many critical tempests.

One disadvantage of this kind of moralizing assumption is that it leads us to neglect (like so many of the post-Ben Jonsonian critics) the curious art-form to which Shakespeare's writings belong: plays written for performance by a theatrical company by one of its life-members. Genetically, a play by Shakespeare is a script written for his actors who by their impersonations will give extra dimensions to the characters. '*Macbeth* has greater affinity with *The Waste Land* than with *The Doll's House*,' L. C. Knights told us in *How Many Children had Lady Macbeth?* a quarter of a century ago, and he still writes as if he believes this. It is as if Dowden or Bradley had said that Shakespeare's plays had greater affinity with *Middlemarch* than with *The Importance of Being Earnest*. (They very nearly did, and that is now their visible defect.) Bradley's modest and sensible view, however, was that the basic way to study Shakespeare was that of the ordinary lovers of the poet who 'read a play more or less as if they were actors who had to study all the parts'.[11] This attitude of mind compares favourably with that of many a modern critic, who does not give the impression of having read the plays more or less as if he were an actor who had to study all the parts.

A lifetime spent in writing for the playhouse developed in Shakespeare his fatal gift of sophistry. As a playwright he learnt the advantage of representing the meeting of ideas in *fair* fight. With increasing artistic virtuosity, he learnt to make, whenever it was convenient, the worse to seem the better cause. He was a Mr. Facing-Bothways. That is why as many religions lay claim to the soul of Shakespeare as Greek cities laid claim to be the birthplace of Homer. That quality of 'flexibility' in Shakespeare's thought which L. C. Knights admires is the very quality that Bernard Shaw found so detestable: 'He used his enormous command of word music to give fascination to his most blackguardly repartees and sublimity to his hollowest platitudes.'[12]

We need not go so far as Bernard Shaw. And even those who find the Shakespearian 'wisdom' too thin, too indeterminate for the twentieth century will admit the probability that 'Shakespeare was trying not merely to represent "life" but to make sense of it, to find meaning and significance'. Still, disillusion with the parson or the politician ought not to send us to Shakespeare; he was more a sophist than a sage.

The nineteenth century felt the importance of Shakespeare as a moral philosopher; one who profoundly explored the springs of human conduct; one who (to use Tennyson's words about the typical

[11] *Shakespearean Tragedy* (1904), p. 2.
[12] *Shaw on Shakespeare*, ed. Edwin Wilson (1962), p. 2.

poet) saw through life and death and saw through his own soul. The moralizers can be seen to have changed in certain ways in the twentieth century. More and more, from reading modern studies of Shakespeare, there emerges the figure of Shakespeare as a Man of Culture, sensitive to the quality of life as it was lived in his day; one who has a taste for the world's great books, such as the Bible and Montaigne and Plutarch, read in a rather sporadic way; also a reader of amusing new books, such as Samuel Harsnet's *Declaration of Popish Impostures*; one with a sense of proportion about the load of knowledge he bears—liable to be ignorant or mistaken about details, of course, such as the penultimate vowels of *misanthropos* and Andronicus, but never going wrong about the big things; well enough but 'not particularly overeducated' (to borrow Charles Dickens's phrase); rather, the Man of Culture in Matthew Arnold's definition, one of those who had succeeded in 'acquainting themselves with the best that has been known and said in the world, and thus with the history of the human spirit'. Observing that much of the best Shakespeare criticism, on both sides of the Atlantic, comes from professional university people, we can declare that the dream of James Russell Lowell has come true. He addressed the Edinburgh Philosophical Institute in 1883, and exclaimed:

> I never open my Shakespeare but what I find myself wishing that there might be professorships established for the study of his works.

It can hardly be denied that there is now a curious tendency for poets and professors to approximate in type. Single-minded poets who were once supposed to have been warbling their native woodnotes wild have been metamorphosed into hard-reading men. The orthodox view of Burns nowadays is, I have heard, that he was a well-read man, not a peasant-poet. Shakespeare, too, has become an author who did a fair amount of research when embarking on a serious new play; a reader who was aware of literature in several languages; it was a *reading knowledge* he had, of course, of foreign languages.

No, we cannot come to Shakespeare with simplicity of mind; too many people have been writing and thinking about Shakespeare for at least three and a half centuries, and the volume of work increases in size and complexity every year. We cannot avoid being influenced by this fact. We shall not approach Shakespeare straight. We have not been influenced only by the great critics of the past and the reputable critics of our own times. Our impressions are conditioned by the literature which has been influenced by Shakespeare. Even if (like Sir Winston Churchill) you have never read *Hamlet*, you still cannot come to it fresh, because *Hamlet* has had its influence upon many other works of literature you *have* read. The great task of criticism is, no doubt, to see the object as it really is. But in order to do this we need to disentangle ourselves from the past as well as, to some extent, from the present. It is corrective to try to see why we have come to feel as we do about Shakespeare in the twentieth century; why we have the characteristic feelings and convinced notions and plausible complexities about Shakespeare that are now part of the critical air we breathe. But this is one of the delightful perils of Shakespeare. The greatest poet is clearly the most dangerous subject of criticism.

IX

The Close of an Epoch

C. V. WEDGWOOD

On 24 March 1603 Queen Elizabeth died. The 'fair vestal throned by the West' who had reigned in England for forty-four years was succeeded on the throne by her cousin the King of Scots—

> Our *omne bonum* from the wholesome North
> Our fruitful Sovereign James.

The quotation is from one of the many laudatory verses offered to the king by his English subjects. The author, Thomas Dekker, was admittedly a purveyor of popular poetry, and therefore one who moved with the times. For him, the new king's journey from his native Scotland into his new realm was a progress accompanied by all the hosts of Heaven:

> Silver crowds
> Of blissful angels and tried martyrs tread
> On the star-ceiling over England's head. . . .[1]

But James VI, King of Scots, who was now James I, King of Great Britain (a name that he hoped would henceforward replace altogether the separate names of England and Scotland), was not accompanied by crowds of blissful angels as he journeyed southwards. He was accompanied by hordes of greedy suitors. In the first unrestrained, and indeed rather endearing, pleasure which he showed at his accession to the long-coveted Crown of England, he lavished honours and prizes with open hands. He was so free with the knighthoods that soon the wits would be referring to the 'cob knights' because like cob nuts they came in clusters. He was also surrounded, as the English courtiers had feared, with a host of Scots who got

[1] *The Non-Dramatic Works of Thomas Dekker,* ed. A. B. Grosart, London, 1884, vol. I, p. 99.

their share—the English said more than their share—of the royal bounty. Later in his reign, with that good humour which was always his most disarming characteristic, King James would say that he had looked upon his first years as a kind of Christmas with presents for all.

As the new king entered into his inheritance the mood in England was one of expectancy, relief and rejoicing. His peaceful accession was in itself a matter for general congratulation, and there was, by and large, less regret for the passing of the great queen and the end of her remarkable reign than hope for the future.

This was natural enough, especially among those who were dependent on the court and ever ready to 'crook the pregnant hinges of the knee' to the current dispensers of favour. They looked for benefits to come from a living king and had no further concern for benefits received from the dead queen; King James had already shown that he responded much more quickly to suitors than the more wary Elizabeth had done. Shakespeare had lived in no other reign than that of Elizabeth, but he knew the common human tendency and had put brief bitter comment on it into the mouth of Hamlet, Prince of Denmark:

> It is not very strange; for my uncle is King of Denmark, and those that would make mows at him while my father lived, give twenty, forty, fifty, an hundred ducats a-piece for his picture in little.
>
> (II. ii. 358ff.)

At the change of sovereigns, he was one of those who remained silent, offering no elegy to the departed Elizabeth, and no poetic welcome to King James. Later on he would include the usual complimentary references to the monarch in his plays. In the closing scene of *King Henry VIII*, James would be compared to a mountain cedar with wide protective branches, and the three weird sisters would mount a pageant for Macbeth indicating the glories of the house of Stuart—'a show of eight Kings, the last with a glass in his hand'. At the third apparition Macbeth had already seen enough—

> Filthy hags!
> Why do you show me this? A fourth! Start, eyes!
> What, will the line stretch out to the crack of doom?
> Another yet! A seventh! I'll see no more:

And yet the eighth appears, who bears a glass
Which shows me many more; and some I see
That two-fold balls and treble sceptres carry . . .
(IV. i. 115ff.)

The glass of the future showed no other successors to the Stuart kings, descended from Banquo, crowned in England as well as Scotland, and ruling also in Ireland; with their double orbs and triple sceptres they marched steadily on. More subtle flattery was contained in Shakespeare's treatment of Banquo, the mythical forefather of King James. The disreputable ruffian of legend, who had been Macbeth's accessory to the murder of Duncan, was metamorphosed into a brave and honourable warrior. Court flattery? Perhaps; but this is also a stroke of genius, for what better foil to the introspective, hag-ridden Macbeth than this open-hearted straightforward gentleman?

The change of sovereigns was to be no loss to Shakespeare. Whatever can be said against the extravagant, often disorderly, sometimes ridiculous court of King James, it was lavish of entertainment and generously appreciative of the theatre. The queen consort, Anne of Denmark, came of an exuberant and gifted family, and shared with her brother, Christian IV, a taste for the more spectacular arts. The reign was to see a series of original and elegant court masques, and the establishment of Inigo Jones as a principal designer of scenery and dresses.

In May 1603 the Lord Chamberlain's Men, with Shakespeare's name mentioned third, became the King's Men, and Shakespeare and his fellow actors marched behind King James on his formal entry into the City of London. In the course of the next decade the court witnessed performances of *Othello*, *Measure for Measure*, *King Lear* and *Macbeth*, the latter being given during the uproarious celebrations which marked the state visit of the Queen's brother, Christian IV, in 1606. At the wedding festivities of the king's daughter Elizabeth, in 1613, no less than seven plays by Shakespeare seem to have been performed at different times—including *Much Ado about Nothing*, *The Winter's Tale*, *The Merry Wives of Windsor*, *Othello* and *Julius Caesar*, as well as the famous and apposite performance of *The Tempest* with its tale of a royal betrothal brought about by the all-wise father of the bride.

We have, for convenience sake, to make divisions in the continuous flow of history. The end of a reign, the end of a dynasty and the end of a century come very close together with the death of Queen Elizabeth I in 1603, which has therefore been selected as a suitable historic milestone. But in the life of Shakespeare, as in the lives of most, if not quite all, Englishmen, the elements of continuity were greater than the elements of change between the two reigns.

Elizabeth's first minister, Robert Cecil, continued to be the first minister of King James, whom he had done his best to prepare for the exacting task of ruling England by some preparatory advice during the last years of Elizabeth's reign. Sir Edward Coke, attorney-general under Elizabeth, continued to serve the Crown as attorney-general under James, and by the zeal of his services, especially in his ferocious manner at the trials of Ralegh and the Gunpowder plotters, gave no inkling of his future activities as the great champion of the Common Law. This later and much more significant part of his career was not to begin until King James had the unfortunate idea of making him Chief Justice of the Common Pleas, where he esteemed it his duty and made it his business to prevent the enroachments of the prerogative courts and the extension of the royal power.

Both Puritans and Roman Catholics were to be disappointed of any radical change in the sovereign's religious policy. The dragging Spanish war was to be concluded in 1604, but the pacific policy of King James was welcome in these early years. Peace had been Queen Elizabeth's desire, when it could be had with safety, and the blessing of peace is a constant theme in Shakespeare's plays which does not alter, and had no need to alter, with the change of sovereign.

The deep and searing changes in English life had come—as Professor Hurstfield has already emphasized—in the generation before Shakespeare was born. Their ultimate consequences might not yet be fully worked out, but at the end of Elizabeth's reign, when Shakespeare was in his fortieth year, there was a relative stability.

King James had frankly looked forward to an easy time in England after his troubled years in Scotland, combating a violent and still powerful nobility and an angrily Calvinist clergy. 'St. George,' he had written, 'surely rides upon a towardly riding horse, while I am daily daunting a wild unruly colt.'[2] His English subjects, too, were at first disposed to welcome the evident advantages of his rule. In the last years of Elizabeth they had never been free from anxiety about the succession or from the fear that her death might be the signal for rebellion at home and possibly invasion from abroad. Once James was securely on the throne these anxieties faded. In place of a childless old woman, the sovereign was now a man in the prime of his life with a growing family of children. The succession ceased to be a problem and the spectre of invasion vanished when the peace with Spain was concluded.

It is true that the union with Scotland was felt to be something of a mixed blessing. Centuries of hostility could not be wiped out in a moment, and relations between the English and the Scots who came into their country seemed at times so bitter that one foreign envoy at least believed that a war between the two nations was ultimately inevitable. While the English resented the presence of Scotsmen seeking their fortunes in England, the Scots had more serious cause for complaint. Their king was now an absentee for years at a time, and where the interests of Scotland and England were at variance, especially in matters of foreign trade and foreign alliances, those of England were inevitably preferred. There were lesser irritations; in the newly designed flag the cross of St. George had been superimposed on the cross of St. Andrew. But England derived one substantial advantage from the union; there was no longer in international affairs any danger of an alliance between Scotland and France.

At the beginning of King James' reign it was not yet apparent that the monarchy as Queen Elizabeth had maintained it was doomed. Parliament had been growing more insistent and more troublesome in its demands, but at no point had the queen lost control of the situation. The elements of future trouble were indeed present, but the problems did not yet appear insoluble. If it was becoming clear that the distribution of power between Crown and Parliament would have to be substantially altered, no one would have foretold that the alteration would plunge the country into civil war.

[2] *Correspondence of James VI with Robert Cecil and others,* ed. J. Bruce, Camden Society, London, 1861, vol. lxxxviii, pp. 31–32.

By the time of Shakespeare's death almost every disastrous element in the situation had fully declared itself; the chronic insolvency of the Crown, the growing aggressiveness of the Commons, the declining prestige of the Dynasty and its servants, and the steady growth of Puritan influence. If we are to talk of the end of an epoch and the beginning of another, this date, 1616, would serve the purpose better than the change of dynasty in 1603.

To solve the perennial problem of finance, Robert Cecil had tried to guide through Parliament a statesmanlike plan known as the Great Contract. The King was to receive a fixed income in return for the surrender of his more irksome feudal rights, especially wardship and purveyance. But the Commons tried to drive too hard a bargain, the King lost patience, and the plan foundered. With the collapse of this plan there was no hope left of any effective solution of the money quarrel between King and Parliament. Both would assert their rights until the crisis of 1640 exploded into Civil War.

Robert Cecil died eighteen months later, and with him ended the succession of loyal, well-informed and judicious ministers who had supported the greatness of the Tudor monarchy. The Stuarts were never to be so fortunate in their servants; they were bad choosers.

In 1613 the King's eldest son, Prince Henry, died. Whether this attractive, headstrong, aggressive young man could have been a successful king in the difficult conditions which lay ahead it is impossible to guess. But he had the popular touch which his father and his younger brother lacked, so that the affection and respect in which the monarchy was traditionally held suffered by his death. King James had retained from his stormy years in Scotland an understandable timorousness of crowds which made him dislike public appearances. His younger son grew up with a fastidious distaste for the common people. Thus, at a time when the personal popularity of the sovereign might have done much to buttress the threatened power of the throne, the royal family tended to withdraw into the private and extravagant world of the Court.

For the court, however admirable in its patronage of the arts, now rapidly acquired a reputation for loose spending and loose living. In the week that Shakespeare died, April 1616, the King was at Royston with his new favourite, George Villiers, later to become Duke of

Buckingham. His previous favourite, Robert Carr, had just been sent to the Tower with his wife, jointly charged with the murder of Thomas Overbury, who had been removed some years earlier to stop him from giving evidence which would have made it impossible for Carr's wife to divorce her previous husband, the Earl of Essex. The King, who, at that time had been foremost in securing the Essex divorce, was now only interested in getting rid of Carr to make way for Villiers. The whole business was squalid and public. It did the Crown no good.

Meanwhile, the King's second Parliament, rightly named the Addled Parliament, had met and had been dissolved after three weeks of arid squabbling. It was clear from this how complete the deadlock between the Commons and the Crown had become. The King, in the unceasing quest for money, had started, cautiously at first but with increasing recklessness, the deplorable practice of selling honours. This he did sometimes directly, sometimes by granting the right to create and sell titles to his favourites. Villiers was to clear nearly twenty-five thousand pounds in Ireland from nine peerages and eleven baronetcies. Irish titles were relatively cheap. The average English peerage began at about twenty thousand, but the price had sunk to about a quarter of this by the end of the reign.

There was nothing new in the steady rise of the wealthy into the ranks of the nobility, but the passage was now easier, and the frankness of the buying and selling brought the Crown rather than the nobility into disrepute. Money and power will always command a certain awe, but the Crown, which was held to be the fountain of honour, became tainted in reputation by this huckstering. James was aware of this; so was his son Charles, but they could not afford to give up the lucrative trade.[3]

The lower ranges of Jacobean society were also fluid; position was acquired by wealth as it had been for the past century. The formalities of social distinctions remained as rigid as ever, and the pleasures of crossing them were not the least reward awaiting the tradesman who made his way up in the world, or married his well-dowered daughters into the aristocracy. The new gentry were probably not so many as the frequency of contemporary comment on them would

[3] Lawrence Stone, 'The Inflation of Honours', *Past and Present*, November, 1958.

lead us to suppose, but they were noticeable. So at the conclusion of *The Winter's Tale* Shakespeare depicts the sudden rise in fortune of two humble folk. The shepherd and his clownish son who had found and brought up the infant Perdita are loaded with honours and fine clothes at the court of her father. The old shepherd says proudly to his son,

> Thy sons and daughters will be all gentlemen born.

The son, gorgeous in his new attire, revels in the humiliation of Autolycus, who had previously twitted him on his low birth:

> You are well met, sir. You denied to fight with me this other day, because I was no gentleman born. See you these clothes? Say you see them not and think me still no gentleman born; you were best say these robes are not gentleman born: give me the lie, do, and try whether I am not now a gentleman born.
>
> *Autolycus.* I know you are now, sir, a gentleman born.
>
> *Clown.* Ay, and have been so any time these four hours.
>
> (V. ii. 124ff.)

While the prestige of the Crown dropped steadily, the danger from the Puritan minority steadily increased. They were estimated by foreign observers to be about a third of the king's subjects. The popular appeal of some of their preachers was by this time a double threat to the theatre. Not only did they preach against players, but the dramatic eloquence of their sermons made the pulpit a competitor of the playhouse. About the time of Shakespeare's death one of London's most popular actors, Nathan Field, protested against the denunciations of the stage currently issuing from the pulpit of St. Mary Overy in Southwark. There was nothing, he argued, positively against acting in the Scriptures, and as His Majesty patronized the stage it was disloyal to denounce it.[4]

But the Privy Council thought it advisable to listen to the protests of the godly from time to time. They forbade one Rossiter to build a new theatre at Puddle Dock because it was so near to Blackfriars Church that the performances would interrupt 'divine service upon

[4] William Haller, *The Rise of Puritanism*, Columbia, 1938, pp. 19ff.; *Calender of State Papers, Domestic Series, 1611–18*, p. 419.

weekdays'. Not long after this the city fathers of Norwich would be appealing to the Council against 'players, tumblers, and such as carry about pageants and shows and the like', on the grounds that entertainments of this kind drew the poorer citizens of Norwich away from 'their works and labours' so that the manufactures, on which they and the town subsisted, were 'in such sort neglected as causeth daily no small loss and damage'.[5]

There had always been a strong undercurrent of opposition to the theatre, with local mayors and justices ready to forbid performances. But by the second decade of the century a measure of popular support was building up behind it. In 1617 a crowd, to the number of many thousands, assembled in Lincoln's Inn Fields and attempted to pull down a playhouse. Such attempts were to be repeated; the crowds involved were usually said to consist of 'loose and lewd persons', but there was an admixture of London apprentices as well as the 'exceeding great multitude of vagrant rogues as there always are about the city'. The influx into London of masterless men from all over the country was an increasingly serious problem. Slums were forming in the suburbs, and it became even more difficult to keep control over the casual labour which accumulated and proliferated round the great seaport.

The London mob was, within a short time of Shakespeare's death, to become a factor in politics. During the clash between King Charles I and his second Parliament over the impeachment of Buckingham in 1626, the Council got wind of a plan to start a riot at the Globe Theatre, and forestalled it in time by closing the theatre on the critical day. Two years later a mob gathered outside the Fortune Theatre and lynched the unfortunate Dr. Lamb, alleged to be Buckingham's tame necromancer, as he came out.[6] These dangerous mixed crowds of apprentices, vagrants and seamen would, a few years later, on the eve of the Civil War, surge round the Parliament house preventing the members they disliked from taking their seats, and would threaten the ill-guarded and vulnerable palace of Whitehall itself.

Less immediately terrible but much more serious in the long run

[5] *Acts of the Privy Council, 1615–16*, p. 292; *1621–3*, pp. 517–18.
[6] S. R. Gardiner, *History of England*, vol. VI, p. 319.

was the growing weight of Puritan opinion among the educated gentry. The late Elizabethan foundation of two markedly Puritan Colleges at Cambridge, Emmanuel and Sidney Sussex, was having its effect both in the ministry and among laymen. It is an odd chance that on the day of Shakespeare's death a tough young gentleman from East Anglia, matriculated at Sidney Sussex—*Oliverius Cromwell Huntingdoniensis.*[7]

Puritanism was the influence which was to make the most immediate modification in the character of English life and politics. But deeper and far more significant changes were beginning over the whole of western Europe. Galileo, born in the same year as Shakespeare, was at the time of his death completing the astronomical observations which were to change the picture of the universe for Western man. Francis Bacon was urging the foundation of a college devoted entirely to the experimental study of the natural sciences. William Harvey was already lecturing in London on the circulation of the blood. The scientific revolution had begun. The close of one epoch marked the beginning of another.

In this last period of Shakespeare's life, what were his compatriots like? Seen through the eyes of visitors to this country our Jacobean ancestors present some unexpected features. Almost all observers agreed that the English were a lively and volatile race. Their self-satisfaction was a byword.

> No nation in Europe is more haughty and insolent nor more conceited of its superior excellence. Were they to be believed, understanding and common sense were to be found only among them. . . .[8]

So wrote the Duc de Sully, ambassador to King James I from Henry IV of France. No doubt he was prejudiced, for as the Venetian envoy noted, 'The English and French hate one another, as is usual between neighbours.'[9]

The frequent corruption of justice and in the management of public affairs shocked this same Venetian deeply. 'Bribery', he wrote,

[7] Abbott, *Writings and Speeches of Oliver Cromwell,* vol. I, p. 27.

[8] *Memoirs of the Duke of Sully*, translated from the French, London, 1778, vol. iii, p. 229.

[9] *Relazioni degli Stati Europei. Lettere al Senato degli Ambasciatori Veneziani nel secolo decimo settimo.* ed. N. Barozzi and G. Berchet, Fourth Series, Venice, 1863, p. 64.

'is the one method for solving all problems in this country.' But he was impressed by the energy of the people, their business acumen, the great fortunes now frequently amassed by English merchants in overseas trade, and the busy and varied shipping which filled the Thames. London Bridge was too narrow for the traffic it had to carry and was always a danger to the boats passing up and down the river and negotiating the rapids under its arches. But it was amusing for foreign visitors to hear the English boasting about their relatives among the heads of traitors exhibited at either end of the Bridge.

Thames transport was well organized and on the whole comfortable, with cushioned seats and coverings against wet weather, and the Thames watermen were extremely skilful—and needed to be. English women were fair and generally pretty, English beer was excellent, and was indeed in demand abroad. The English were reputed good soldiers, but liked their comforts and were therefore not so good as the Scots; they were good sailors, but better pirates.[10]

Apart from the proud conviction that there was no place or people better than England and the English in the world, the national character is not instantly recognizable from these accounts of the earlier seventeenth century. The impression is of a noisier, gayer, more fickle, more demonstrative people than we have since become. They like noise, one foreigner reported, and will go into a church and ring the bells simply for fun.

Their skill as actors was famous and English strolling players were popular abroad. The fact that they delighted foreign audiences indicates their liveliness, energy and skill in mime, for their language was not widely understood. Though English acting was admired, the English language was not. This awkward mixture of Saxon and French—as it seemed to visitors—could sometimes sound attractive when spoken by the natives. But it was not a language that an educated man needed to acquire. Foreigners engaged in trade mastered it when necessary, but diplomatic representatives, however long resident in the country, rarely took the trouble. Though they often reported with pleasure dramatic representations at Court and elsewhere, the treasures of the language were poured out for them in vain. They remained unaware that they were listening to one of

[10] *Ibid.*, pp. 27–30, 92–93.

the richest languages of the world at its greatest moment. Had they been told so, they would no doubt have thought it another absurd manifestation of English conceit.

But the English themselves—their writers at least—were very well pleased with their language. They praised its rhythmic qualities, its mingling of strong consonants and open vowels, its wealth of forceful monosyllables, and the huge variety of its idioms. Its flexibility and beauty, its fitness for all and every subject, were continually demonstrated by poets, dramatists and translators. It was the era of the great dictionaries—Florio's Italian Dictionary, Cotgrave's French Dictionary, Minsheu's Spanish and polyglot Dictionaries; all these bore witness to the inexhaustible variety of English and its capacity to express every shade of meaning.

Such a language had a great future, as Samuel Daniel predicted in lines which have become famous:

> And who in time knows whither we may vent
> The treasure of our tongue? To what strange shores
> This gain of our best glory shall be sent
> T'enrich unknowing nations with our stores?
> What worlds in th' yet unformed occident
> May come refin'd with th'accents that are ours?[11]

Certainly there was poetry now being written in English that would in time to come circle the globe—

> How sweet the moonlight sleeps upon this bank!
> Here will we sit, and let the sounds of music
> Creep in our ears: soft stillness and the night
> Become the touches of sweet harmony.
> Sit, Jessica. Look how the floor of Heaven
> Is thick inlaid with patines of bright gold:
> There's not the smallest orb which thou behold'st
> But in his motion like an angel sings,
> Still quiring to the young-eyed cherubins;
> Such harmony is in immortal souls;
> But whilst this muddy vesture of decay
> Doth grossly close it in, we cannot hear it.
>
> (*M. of V.*, V. i. 54ff.)

Such lines are for all time, and it is strange to think that they were

[11] *The Complete Works of Samuel Daniel*, ed. A. B. Grosart, 1885, vol. I, p. 255.

written in a language of small circulation and less prestige, for a public, enthusiastic and appreciative indeed, but limited to the town-dwelling, theatre-going minority of a country at that time only on the perimeter of the intellectual world.

The expansion had already begun. The treasure of the tongue that Shakespeare spoke was already reaching strange shores, especially in the yet unformed occident, which English enterprise was doing its best to form to its own heart's desire. The Virginian colony was struggling to establish itself. It was in the year of Shakespeare's death that the Indian princess Pocahontas was received at court and became the talk of the town. Soon the poet and colonial venturer George Sandys would spend his leisure time, among the dangers and hardships of life in Virginia, translating the Metamorphoses of Ovid into English verse—the first work of English literature to be produced in America.

Shakespeare himself had been inspired by the misadventures of the Virginian colonists in the setting of *The Tempest*. In 1609 a fleet bound for Virginia was scattered by a storm of unexampled fury. It was thus described by a survivor:

> An hell of darkness turned black upon us . . . we could not apprehend in our imaginations any possibility of greater violence, yet did we still find it, not only more terrible but more constant, fury added to fury, and one storm urging a second more outragious than the former . . . our clamours drowned in the winds and the winds in thunder. Prayers might well be in the hearts and lips but drowned in the outcry of the officers. . . . The sea swelled above the clouds and gave battle unto Heaven. It could not be said to rain, the water like whole rivers did flood in the air. . . . Upon Thursday night Sir George Summers being upon the watch, had an apparition of a little round light, like a faint star, trembling and streaming along with a sparkling blaze, half the height upon the main mast, and shooting sometimes from shroud to shroud, tempting to settle as it were upon any of the four shrouds; and for three or four hours together, or rather more, running sometimes along the main yard to the very end and then returning . . .[12]

This scene of darkness, storm and dismay, lit by St. Elmo's fire, is very close to the storm so wonderfully conjured up in the opening

[12] *The Tempest*, Arden edition, London, 1954, Appendix A.

scene of *The Tempest* and later described, as a spectator by the frightened Miranda, and as the agent of the storm by Ariel. Thus Miranda

> If by your art, my dearest father, you have
> Put the wild waters in this roar, allay them.
> The sky, it seems, would pour down stinking pitch,
> But that the sea, mounting to the welkin's cheek,
> Dashes the fire out. . . .
>
> (I. ii. 1ff.)

and later Ariel:

> I boarded the King's ship; now on the beak,
> Now in the waist, the deck, in every cabin,
> I flamed amazement; sometime I'ld divide,
> And burn in many places; on the topmast,
> The yards and bowsprit would I flame distinctly,
> Then meet and join. Jove's lightnings, the precursors
> O' the dreadful thunder claps, more momentary
> And sight-outrunning were not; the fire and cracks
> Of sulphurous roaring the most mighty Neptune
> Seem to besiege, and make his bold waves tremble,
> Yea, his dread trident shake.
>
> (I. ii. 196ff.)

The storm-tossed adventurers had already given themselves over for lost, when Sir George Summers saw land, and they ran ashore off an island. This turned out to be one of 'the dangerous and dreaded islands of the Bermuda', believed to be inhabited by devils and therefore 'feared and avoided of all sea travellers alive above any other place in the world'. But on further investigation they found this 'most prodigious and enchanted place' to be little short of an earthly paradise, abounding in food of all kinds, fish, fruit, hogs and turtles. Here they were able to refresh themselves plentifully, to build new ships, and proceed in the spring to Virginia.

Thus Shakespeare's last play, with its visionary dreamlike quality and theme of reconciliation, is linked to the true story of the misfortunes and deliverance of the Virginian colonists. Shakespeare had a vicarious interest in the venture through several of his friends, and it is as certain as such things can be that the accounts he read of the adventure, in print and in manuscript, inspired him to the setting and the dramatic opening of this play. But in his use of the material, the old and the new world, the past and the future have been marvellously combined. He uses the details of the shipwreck off the 'still vexed Bermoothes', but he sets his own enchanted island back in the old world, in the Mediterranean between Naples and the African coast.

There is something impertinent in attempting to attach the life and world of so transcendant a genius to the commonplaces of economic or social history. None the less, the outline of Shakespeare's life and career is in harmony with this period of expansion and social change. He can be seen as a man of the sixteenth century whose mind responded to the times, who built up his position in the world and acquired possessions and social status as he acquired wealth. He accumulated a competent fortune; in his later life he lived well, bought the best house in Stratford and ended his days as its most distinguished citizen. Very soon after his death, passing visitors would be proudly shown in his parish Church 'a neat monument of the most famous English poet Mr. William Shakespeare'.

But changes were happening in the Stratford that Shakespeare knew. Within a few years the River Avon, in Shakespeare's time not navigable by 'a boat of any burden', would be made passable from Tewkesbury to Stratford for barges of thirty tons.[13] The iron manufacture of Birmingham was growing steadily. In the Civil War it would be supplying swords—not very good ones, these 'Brummagem blades'—to whichever side happened to have gained control of it.

Changes in fashion and taste were meanwhile altering the theatre. With the lessening respect for the Crown, dramatists and players became bolder in handling contemporary themes. There was the extraordinary daring of Middleton's *A Game at Chess*, a savage attack on the king's policy of Spanish marriage for his son, against which the Spanish ambassador protested. But the court was out of London, and the play ran to packed houses for eleven nights before it was ordered to be taken off.[14]

This ferocious political play was a sign of the times; if few play-

[13] W. H. B. Court, *Rise of the Midland Industries, 1600–1838*, Oxford, 1938, p. 10.
[14] *Acts of the Privy Council, 1623–24*, p. 305; Leslie Hotson, *Shakespeare's Wooden O*, London, 1959, pp. 16ff.

wrights ventured quite so far as this, the fashion was now all for plays about matters of immediate and mostly ephemeral interest. The generation after Shakespeare's death produced a stream of social comedies on currently popular topics, of value to historians, but rarely of any permanent quality. Aubrey was in the right of it when he contrasted these playwrights to their disparagement with Shakespeare: 'His comedies will remain wit as long as the English tongue is understood, for that he handles *mores hominum*. Now our present writers reflect so much upon particular persons and coxcombeities that twenty years hence they will not be understood.'[15]

Shakespeare was as acutely conscious as any good dramatist must be of the tastes and fashions of his day. He spoke of actors as 'the abstracts and brief chronicles of the time'. But the topical and personal allusions in his plays are incidental, never structural. Yet it can perhaps be argued that the creeping political uncertainty of King James's reign is reflected in the atmosphere of the later plays wherever these touch on political themes or on the exercise of human power which is the stuff of politics.

Professor Hurstfield has pointed out that Shakespeare was as deeply concerned as any respectable citizen must be for the good government of his country. Growing up under the shadow of disturbing changes, reaching his maturity at a time when the threat of foreign invasion was real and the national danger a constant preoccupation, his recurrent themes are the necessity of strong and *legal* government. The House of Lancaster falls because of this basic flaw in its right, in spite of the triumphant interlude of King Henry V. Above all, Shakespeare prizes the blessings of peace. The great dramatic epic that he devoted to the Wars of the Roses, their causes and their cure, was essentially an indictment of civil war as the worst of disasters.

The political themes of his later plays are less consistent and more disillusioned. Octavius, who should be the Henry VII of the Roman civil wars, is treated in such a way as to alienate sympathy and discourage admiration. One feels that Shakespeare's political judgement is divided, or rather, that his understanding of individuals is now so mature and so perceptive that the simple handling of a political

[15] *Aubrey's Brief Lives*, ed. Oliver Lawson Dick, London, 1949, p. 276.

theme is too coarse for him. These plays have politics in them, but they are not about politics; they are about people.

Is it too fanciful to suggest that a mounting political disillusion, a disillusion about the nature of human power, can be traced not only in the Roman plays, but also in *Macbeth*, in *Othello*, most strongly of all in *King Lear*? The intractability of the problem of regal power was becoming evident in the England of Shakespeare's maturity; the dangers were growing. The indications are necessarily vague, but the political uneasiness of the later plays is in sharp contrast to the clear political line of his earlier work.

Twenty-five years divided the death of Shakespeare from the foundering of his country into a second Civil War, a war which—both for the principles involved and the character of the protagonists—would have provided better material for Shakespeare's genius than the baronial struggles of the fifteenth century. During that interval his plays continued to hold the stage and, with their publication, to delight readers. We find a young English courtier travelling in Italy with 'Shaxper's book' for a companion. At Venice he crossed one afternoon to San Giorgio—'St. George's' he calls it—and spent the afternoon with a friend reading in the book. They must have been reading aloud to each other, since only one book is mentioned—there in the sunny cloister in the lagoon, declaiming the uncouth language which the Italians despised, and in which some of the loveliest poetry in the world had been created.[16]

A few years later, a harassed Civil Servant, struggling to shore up the fast collapsing Government of Charles I, with too many calls on his time and too little help, protests to a friend that he cannot 'play Pyramus and Thisbe and the Lion, too'.[17] Soon after, Queen Henrietta Maria, marching down from the North with arms and supplies for her husband—a gayer and less vindictive Margaret of Anjou—will pass the night at Stratford, at New Place, as the guest of Shakespeare's daughter. Later, the king, a prisoner at Holmby House, will read the plays for recreation and annotate his folio here and there in his delicate neat handwriting. At a still grimmer moment in the struggle John Cook, the attorney-general, preparing to arraign the

[16] Helen Kaufman, *Conscientious Cavalier*, London, 1962, p. 137.
[17] *Calendar of State Papers, Domestic Series, 1639*, p. 272.

King in the name of 'my clients the people of England', will brood over the rumoured poisoning of King James by Buckingham and the unwillingness of Charles to investigate the matter. Had the king read the Scriptures more, and Shakespeare less, wrote Cook with vindictive glee, he would have known that it was his duty to avenge his father's death.[18] Had John Cook known his Shakespeare as he knew his Bible he might have remembered Hamlet.

With the changed taste of the Restoration, Shakespeare came back to the stage, played in a different manner and sometimes in an altered text. The women's parts were now played by women. Prince Rupert, stern veteran of wars by land and sea, fell in love with the first recorded Desdemona, ash-blonde Margaret Hughes with her soft Welsh voice, wooed her and made her his own—

> She loved me for the dangers I had passed,
> And I loved her that she did pity them. . . .

A little later Dryden offered his amended version of *The Tempest* to the sophisticated Restoration audience, with some apology for refurbishing this old-fashioned stuff—

> As when a tree's cut down the secret root
> Lives under ground, and thence new branches shoot;
> So from old Shakespeare's honoured dust, this day
> Springs up and buds a new reviving play. . . .

Dryden was too good a poet and too good a critic not to reverence Shakespeare, but he felt that the magical element in the plot needed some excuse in the age of the newly founded Royal Society, of Christopher Wren and Robert Boyle and Isaac Newton.

> I must confess 'twas bold, nor would you now
> That liberty to vulgar wits allow,
> Which works by magic supernatural things . . .
> Those legends from old priesthood were received,
> And he then writ as people then believed . . . .

What Shakespeare believed or did not believe is matter for speculation still. He does not work by supernatural, but by natural magic. Today, when the Scientific Revolution, just beginning when he died, has wrought unimaginable changes in every sphere of thought,

[18] John Cook, *King Charles His Case*, London, 1649.

in every corner of our lives, his magic still works. He speaks to us differently, but no less truly than he did to our ancestors in the England of King James and Queen Elizabeth I.

Before beauty and truth of such depth and harmony, historical reflections on the nature of an epoch and the poet's relation to it, seem irrelevant—

> The cloud-capp'd towers, the gorgeous palaces,
> The solemn temples, the great globe itself,
> Yea, all which it inherit, shall dissolve,
> And, like this insubstantial pageant faded,
> Leave not a rack behind. We are such stuff
> As dreams are made on; and our little life
> Is rounded with a sleep.

Index

For Shakespeare's Works, see overleaf.

Shakespeare's Works

Index of References to Shakespeare's Works cited in the text by name, character in play or quotation.